Big Data Analytics with R and Hadoop

Set up an integrated infrastructure of R and Hadoop to turn your data analytics into Big Data analytics

Vignesh Prajapati

[PACKT] open source*
PUBLISHING   community experience distilled

BIRMINGHAM - MUMBAI

Big Data Analytics with R and Hadoop

First published: November 2013

Production Reference: 1181113

Published by Packt Publishing Ltd.
Livery Place
35 Livery Street
Birmingham B3 2PB, UK.

ISBN 978-1-78216-328-2

www.packtpub.com

Cover Image by Duraid Fatouhi (duraidfatouhi@yahoo.com)

Credits

Author
Vignesh Prajapati

Reviewers
Krishnanand Khambadkone
Muthusamy Manigandan
Vidyasagar N V
Siddharth Tiwari

Acquisition Editor
James Jones

Lead Technical Editor
Mandar Ghate

Technical Editors
Shashank Desai
Jinesh Kampani
Chandni Maishery

Project Coordinator
Wendell Palmar

Copy Editors
Roshni Banerjee
Mradula Hegde
Insiya Morbiwala
Aditya Nair
Kirti Pai
Shambhavi Pai
Laxmi Subramanian

Proofreaders
Maria Gould
Lesley Harrison
Elinor Perry-Smith

Indexer
Mariammal Chettiyar

Graphics
Ronak Dhruv
Abhinash Sahu

Production Coordinator
Pooja Chiplunkar

Cover Work
Pooja Chiplunkar

About the Author

Vignesh Prajapati, from India, is a Big Data enthusiast, a Pingax (www.pingax.com) consultant and a software professional at Enjay. He is an experienced ML Data engineer. He is experienced with Machine learning and Big Data technologies such as R, Hadoop, Mahout, Pig, Hive, and related Hadoop components to analyze datasets to achieve informative insights by data analytics cycles.

He pursued B.E from Gujarat Technological University in 2012 and started his career as Data Engineer at Tatvic. His professional experience includes working on the development of various Data analytics algorithms for Google Analytics data source, for providing economic value to the products. To get the ML in action, he implemented several analytical apps in collaboration with Google Analytics and Google Prediction API services. He also contributes to the R community by developing the RGoogleAnalytics' R library as an open source code Google project and writes articles on Data-driven technologies.

Vignesh is not limited to a single domain; he has also worked for developing various interactive apps via various Google APIs, such as Google Analytics API, Realtime API, Google Prediction API, Google Chart API, and Translate API with the Java and PHP platforms. He is highly interested in the development of open source technologies.

Vignesh has also reviewed the Apache Mahout Cookbook for Packt Publishing. This book provides a fresh, scope-oriented approach to the Mahout world for beginners as well as advanced users. Mahout Cookbook is specially designed to make users aware of the different possible machine learning applications, strategies, and algorithms to produce an intelligent as well as Big Data application.

Acknowledgment

First and foremost, I would like to thank my loving parents and younger brother Vaibhav for standing beside me throughout my career as well as while writing this book. Without their support it would have been totally impossible to achieve this knowledge sharing. As I started writing this book, I was continuously motivated by my father (Prahlad Prajapati) and regularly followed up by my mother (Dharmistha Prajapati). Also, thanks to my friends for encouraging me to initiate writing for big technologies such as Hadoop and R.

During this writing period I went through some critical phases of my life, which were challenging for me at all times. I am grateful to Ravi Pathak, CEO and founder at Tatvic, who introduced me to this vast field of Machine learning and Big Data and helped me realize my potential. And yes, I can't forget James, Wendell, and Mandar from Packt Publishing for their valuable support, motivation, and guidance to achieve these heights. Special thanks to them for filling up the communication gap on the technical and graphical sections of this book.

Thanks to Big Data and Machine learning. Finally a big thanks to God, you have given me the power to believe in myself and pursue my dreams. I could never have done this without the faith I have in you, the Almighty.

Let us go forward together into the future of Big Data analytics.

About the Reviewers

Krishnanand Khambadkone has over 20 years of overall experience. He is currently working as a senior solutions architect in the Big Data and Hadoop Practice of TCS America and is architecting and implementing Hadoop solutions for Fortune 500 clients, mainly large banking organizations. Prior to this he worked on delivering middleware and SOA solutions using the Oracle middleware stack and built and delivered software using the J2EE product stack.

He is an avid evangelist and enthusiast of Big Data and Hadoop. He has written several articles and white papers on this subject, and has also presented these at conferences.

Muthusamy Manigandan is the Head of Engineering and Architecture with Ozone Media. Mani has more than 15 years of experience in designing large-scale software systems in the areas of virtualization, Distributed Version Control systems, ERP, supply chain management, Machine Learning and Recommendation Engine, behavior-based retargeting, and behavior targeting creative. Prior to joining Ozone Media, Mani handled various responsibilities at VMware, Oracle, AOL, and Manhattan Associates. At Ozone Media he is responsible for products, technology, and research initiatives. Mani can be reached at mmaniga@ yahoo.co.uk and http://in.linkedin.com/in/mmanigandan/.

Vidyasagar N V had an interest in computer science since an early age. Some of his serious work in computers and computer networks began during his high school days. Later he went to the prestigious Institute Of Technology, Banaras Hindu University for his B.Tech. He is working as a software developer and data expert, developing and building scalable systems. He has worked with a variety of second, third, and fourth generation languages. He has also worked with flat files, indexed files, hierarchical databases, network databases, and relational databases, such as NOSQL databases, Hadoop, and related technologies. Currently, he is working as a senior developer at Collective Inc., developing Big-Data-based structured data extraction techniques using the web and local information. He enjoys developing high-quality software, web-based solutions, and designing secure and scalable data systems.

I would like to thank my parents, Mr. N Srinivasa Rao and Mrs. Latha Rao, and my family who supported and backed me throughout my life, and friends for being friends. I would also like to thank all those people who willingly donate their time, effort, and expertise by participating in open source software projects. Thanks to Packt Publishing for selecting me as one of the technical reviewers on this wonderful book. It is my honor to be a part of this book. You can contact me at `vidyasagar1729@gmail.com`.

Siddharth Tiwari has been in the industry since the past three years working on Machine learning, Text Analytics, Big Data Management, and information search and Management. Currently he is employed by EMC Corporation's Big Data management and analytics initiative and product engineering wing for their Hadoop distribution.

He is a part of the TeraSort and MinuteSort world records, achieved while working with a large financial services firm.

He pursued Bachelor of Technology from Uttar Pradesh Technical University with equivalent CGPA 8.

www.PacktPub.com

Support files, eBooks, discount offers and more

You might want to visit www.PacktPub.com for support files and downloads related to your book.

Did you know that Packt offers eBook versions of every book published, with PDF and ePub files available? You can upgrade to the eBook version at www.PacktPub.com and as a print book customer, you are entitled to a discount on the eBook copy. Get in touch with us at service@packtpub.com for more details.

At www.PacktPub.com, you can also read a collection of free technical articles, sign up for a range of free newsletters and receive exclusive discounts and offers on Packt books and eBooks.

http://PacktLib.PacktPub.com

Do you need instant solutions to your IT questions? PacktLib is Packt's online digital book library. Here, you can access, read and search across Packt's entire library of books.

Why Subscribe?

- Fully searchable across every book published by Packt
- Copy and paste, print and bookmark content
- On demand and accessible via web browser

Free Access for Packt account holders

If you have an account with Packt at www.PacktPub.com, you can use this to access PacktLib today and view nine entirely free books. Simply use your login credentials for immediate access.

Table of Contents

Preface

The volume of data that enterprises acquire every day is increasing exponentially. It is now possible to store these vast amounts of information on low cost platforms such as Hadoop.

The conundrum these organizations now face is what to do with all this data and how to glean key insights from this data. Thus R comes into picture. R is a very amazing tool that makes it a snap to run advanced statistical models on data, translate the derived models into colorful graphs and visualizations, and do a lot more functions related to data science.

One key drawback of R, though, is that it is not very scalable. The core R engine can process and work on very limited amount of data. As Hadoop is very popular for Big Data processing, corresponding R with Hadoop for scalability is the next logical step.

This book is dedicated to R and Hadoop and the intricacies of how data analytics operations of R can be made scalable by using a platform as Hadoop.

With this agenda in mind, this book will cater to a wide audience including data scientists, statisticians, data architects, and engineers who are looking for solutions to process and analyze vast amounts of information using R and Hadoop.

Using R with Hadoop will provide an elastic data analytics platform that will scale depending on the size of the dataset to be analyzed. Experienced programmers can then write Map/Reduce modules in R and run it using Hadoop's parallel processing Map/Reduce mechanism to identify patterns in the dataset.

Introducing R

R is an open source software package to perform statistical analysis on data. R is a programming language used by data scientist statisticians and others who need to make statistical analysis of data and glean key insights from data using mechanisms, such as regression, clustering, classification, and text analysis. R is registered under **GNU** (**General Public License**). It was developed by Ross Ihaka and Robert Gentleman at the University of Auckland, New Zealand, which is currently handled by the R Development Core Team. It can be considered as a different implementation of S, developed by Johan Chambers at Bell Labs. There are some important differences, but a lot of the code written in S can be unaltered using the R interpreter engine.

R provides a wide variety of statistical, machine learning (linear and nonlinear modeling, classic statistical tests, time-series analysis, classification, clustering) and graphical techniques, and is highly extensible. R has various built-in as well as extended functions for statistical, machine learning, and visualization tasks such as:

- Data extraction
- Data cleaning
- Data loading
- Data transformation
- Statistical analysis
- Predictive modeling
- Data visualization

It is one of the most popular open source statistical analysis packages available on the market today. It is crossplatform, has a very wide community support, and a large and ever-growing user community who are adding new packages every day. With its growing list of packages, R can now connect with other data stores, such as MySQL, SQLite, MongoDB, and Hadoop for data storage activities.

Understanding features of R

Let's see different useful features of R:

- Effective programming language
- Relational database support
- Data analytics
- Data visualization
- Extension through the vast library of R packages

Studying the popularity of R

The graph provided from KD suggests that R is the most popular language for data analysis and mining:

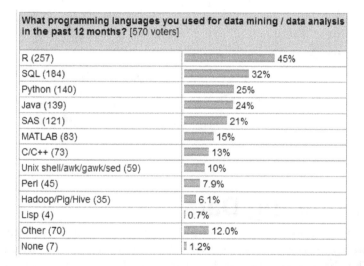

What programming languages you used for data mining / data analysis in the past 12 months? [570 voters]	
R (257)	45%
SQL (184)	32%
Python (140)	25%
Java (139)	24%
SAS (121)	21%
MATLAB (83)	15%
C/C++ (73)	13%
Unix shell/awk/gawk/sed (59)	10%
Perl (45)	7.9%
Hadoop/Pig/Hive (35)	6.1%
Lisp (4)	0.7%
Other (70)	12.0%
None (7)	1.2%

The following graph provides details about the total number of R packages released by R users from 2005 to 2013. This is how we explore R users. The growth was exponential in 2012 and it seems that 2013 is on track to beat that.

R allows performing Data analytics by various statistical and machine learning operations as follows:

- Regression
- Classification
- Clustering
- Recommendation
- Text mining

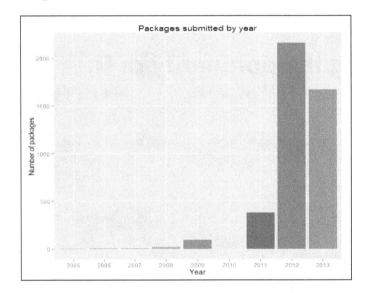

Introducing Big Data

Big Data has to deal with large and complex datasets that can be structured, semi-structured, or unstructured and will typically not fit into memory to be processed. They have to be processed in place, which means that computation has to be done where the data resides for processing. When we talk to developers, the people actually building Big Data systems and applications, we get a better idea of what they mean about 3Vs. They typically would mention the 3Vs model of Big Data, which are velocity, volume, and variety.

Velocity refers to the low latency, real-time speed at which the analytics need to be applied. A typical example of this would be to perform analytics on a continuous stream of data originating from a social networking site or aggregation of disparate sources of data.

Volume refers to the size of the dataset. It may be in KB, MB, GB, TB, or PB based on the type of the application that generates or receives the data.

Variety refers to the various types of the data that can exist, for example, text, audio, video, and photos.

Big Data usually includes datasets with sizes. It is not possible for such systems to process this amount of data within the time frame mandated by the business. Big Data volumes are a constantly moving target, as of 2012 ranging from a few dozen terabytes to many petabytes of data in a single dataset. Faced with this seemingly insurmountable challenge, entirely new platforms are called Big Data platforms.

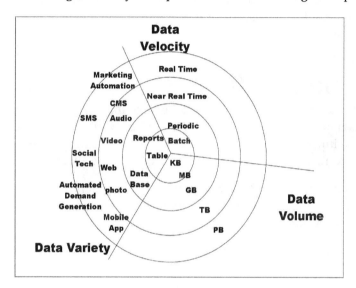

Getting information about popular organizations that hold Big Data

Some of the popular organizations that hold Big Data are as follows:

- Facebook: It has 40 PB of data and captures 100 TB/day
- Yahoo!: It has 60 PB of data
- Twitter: It captures 8 TB/day
- EBay: It has 40 PB of data and captures 50 TB/day

How much data is considered as Big Data differs from company to company. Though true that one company's Big Data is another's small, there is something common: doesn't fit in memory, nor disk, has rapid influx of data that needs to be processed and would benefit from distributed software stacks. For some companies, 10 TB of data would be considered Big Data and for others 1 PB would be Big Data. So only you can determine whether the data is really Big Data. It is sufficient to say that it would start in the low terabyte range.

Also, a question well worth asking is, as you are not capturing and retaining enough of your data do you think you do not have a Big Data problem now? In some scenarios, companies literally discard data, because there wasn't a cost effective way to store and process it. With platforms as Hadoop, it is possible to start capturing and storing all that data.

Introducing Hadoop

Apache Hadoop is an open source Java framework for processing and querying vast amounts of data on large clusters of commodity hardware. Hadoop is a top level Apache project, initiated and led by Yahoo! and Doug Cutting. It relies on an active community of contributors from all over the world for its success.

With a significant technology investment by Yahoo!, Apache Hadoop has become an enterprise-ready cloud computing technology. It is becoming the industry de facto framework for Big Data processing.

Hadoop changes the economics and the dynamics of large-scale computing. Its impact can be boiled down to four salient characteristics. Hadoop enables scalable, cost-effective, flexible, fault-tolerant solutions.

Exploring Hadoop features

Apache Hadoop has two main features:

- HDFS (Hadoop Distributed File System)
- MapReduce

Studying Hadoop components

Hadoop includes an ecosystem of other products built over the core HDFS and MapReduce layer to enable various types of operations on the platform. A few popular Hadoop components are as follows:

- **Mahout**: This is an extensive library of machine learning algorithms.

- **Pig**: Pig is a high-level language (such as PERL) to analyze large datasets with its own language syntax for expressing data analysis programs, coupled with infrastructure for evaluating these programs.

- **Hive**: Hive is a data warehouse system for Hadoop that facilitates easy data summarization, ad hoc queries, and the analysis of large datasets stored in HDFS. It has its own SQL-like query language called **Hive Query Language (HQL)**, which is used to issue query commands to Hadoop.

- **HBase**: **HBase (Hadoop Database)** is a distributed, column-oriented database. HBase uses HDFS for the underlying storage. It supports both batch style computations using MapReduce and atomic queries (random reads).

- **Sqoop**: Apache Sqoop is a tool designed for efficiently transferring bulk data between Hadoop and Structured Relational Databases. **Sqoop** is an abbreviation for **(SQ)**L to Had**(oop)**.

- **ZooKeper**: ZooKeeper is a centralized service to maintain configuration information, naming, providing distributed synchronization, and group services, which are very useful for a variety of distributed systems.

- **Ambari**: A web-based tool for provisioning, managing, and monitoring Apache Hadoop clusters, which includes support for Hadoop HDFS, Hadoop MapReduce, Hive, HCatalog, HBase, ZooKeeper, Oozie, Pig, and Sqoop.

Understanding the reason for using R and Hadoop together

I would also say that sometimes the data resides on the HDFS (in various formats). Since a lot of data analysts are very productive in R, it is natural to use R to compute with the data stored through Hadoop-related tools.

As mentioned earlier, the strengths of R lie in its ability to analyze data using a rich library of packages but fall short when it comes to working on very large datasets. The strength of Hadoop on the other hand is to store and process very large amounts of data in the TB and even PB range. Such vast datasets cannot be processed in memory as the RAM of each machine cannot hold such large datasets. The options would be to run analysis on limited chunks also known as sampling or to correspond the analytical power of R with the storage and processing power of Hadoop and you arrive at an ideal solution. Such solutions can also be achieved in the cloud using platforms such as Amazon EMR.

What this book covers

Chapter 1, Getting Ready to Use R and Hadoop, gives an introduction as well as the process of installing R and Hadoop.

Chapter 2, Writing Hadoop MapReduce Programs, covers basics of Hadoop MapReduce and ways to execute MapReduce using Hadoop.

Chapter 3, Integrating R and Hadoop, shows deployment and running of sample MapReduce programs for RHadoop and RHIPE by various data handling processes.

Chapter 4, Using Hadoop Streaming with R, shows how to use Hadoop Streaming with R.

Chapter 5, Learning Data Analytics with R and Hadoop, introduces the Data analytics project life cycle by demonstrating with real-world Data analytics problems.

Chapter 6, Understanding Big Data Analysis with Machine Learning, covers performing Big Data analytics by machine learning techniques with RHadoop.

Chapter 7, Importing and Exporting Data from Various DBs, covers how to interface with popular relational databases to import and export data operations with R.

Appendix, References, describes links to additional resources regarding the content of all the chapters being present.

What you need for this book

As we are going to perform Big Data analytics with R and Hadoop, you should have basic knowledge of R and Hadoop and how to perform the practicals and you will need to have R and Hadoop installed and configured. It would be great if you already have a larger size data and problem definition that can be solved with data-driven technologies, such as R and Hadoop functions.

Who this book is for

This book is great for R developers who are looking for a way to perform Big Data analytics with Hadoop. They would like all the techniques of integrating R and Hadoop, how to write Hadoop MapReduce, and tutorials for developing and running Hadoop MapReduce within R. Also this book is aimed at those who know Hadoop and want to build some intelligent applications over Big Data with R packages. It would be helpful if readers have basic knowledge of R.

Conventions

In this book, you will find a number of styles of text that distinguish between different kinds of information. Here are some examples of these styles, and an explanation of their meaning.

Code words in text, database table names, folder names, filenames, file extensions, pathnames, dummy URLs, user input, and Twitter handles are shown as follows: "Preparing the `Map()` input."

A block of code is set as follows:

```
<property>
<name>mapred.job.tracker</name>
<value>localhost:54311</value>
<description>The host and port that the MapReduce job tracker runs
at. If "local", then jobs are run in-process as a single map
and reduce task.
</description>
</property>
```

Any command-line input or output is written as follows:

```
// Setting the environment variables for running Java and Hadoop commands
export HADOOP_HOME=/usr/local/hadoop
export JAVA_HOME=/usr/lib/jvm/java-6-sun
```

New terms and **important words** are shown in bold. Words that you see on the screen, in menus or dialog boxes for example, appear in the text like this: "Open the **Password** tab. ".

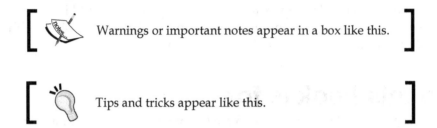

Warnings or important notes appear in a box like this.

Tips and tricks appear like this.

Reader feedback

Feedback from our readers is always welcome. Let us know what you think about this book—what you liked or may have disliked. Reader feedback is important for us to develop titles that you really get the most out of.

To send us general feedback, simply send an e-mail to feedback@packtpub.com, and mention the book title via the subject of your message.

If there is a topic that you have expertise in and you are interested in either writing or contributing to a book, see our author guide on www.packtpub.com/authors.

Customer support

Now that you are the proud owner of a Packt book, we have a number of things to help you to get the most from your purchase.

Downloading the example code

You can download the example code files for all Packt books you have purchased from your account at http://www.packtpub.com. If you purchased this book elsewhere, you can visit http://www.packtpub.com/support and register to have the files e-mailed directly to you.

Errata

Although we have taken every care to ensure the accuracy of our content, mistakes do happen. If you find a mistake in one of our books—maybe a mistake in the text or the code—we would be grateful if you would report this to us. By doing so, you can save other readers from frustration and help us improve subsequent versions of this book. If you find any errata, please report them by visiting `http://www.packtpub.com/submit-errata`, selecting your book, clicking on the **errata submission form** link, and entering the details of your errata. Once your errata are verified, your submission will be accepted and the errata will be uploaded on our website, or added to any list of existing errata, under the Errata section of that title. Any existing errata can be viewed by selecting your title from `http://www.packtpub.com/support`.

Piracy

Piracy of copyright material on the Internet is an ongoing problem across all media. At Packt, we take the protection of our copyright and licenses very seriously. If you come across any illegal copies of our works, in any form, on the Internet, please provide us with the location address or website name immediately so that we can pursue a remedy.

Please contact us at `copyright@packtpub.com` with a link to the suspected pirated material.

We appreciate your help in protecting our authors, and our ability to bring you valuable content.

Questions

You can contact us at `questions@packtpub.com` if you are having a problem with any aspect of the book, and we will do our best to address it.

1
Getting Ready to Use R and Hadoop

The first chapter has been bundled with several topics on R and Hadoop basics as follows:

- R Installation, features, and data modeling
- Hadoop installation, features, and components

In the preface, we introduced you to R and Hadoop. This chapter will focus on getting you up and running with these two technologies. Until now, R has been used mainly for statistical analysis, but due to the increasing number of functions and packages, it has become popular in several fields, such as machine learning, visualization, and data operations. R will not load all data (Big Data) into machine memory. So, Hadoop can be chosen to load the data as Big Data. Not all algorithms work across Hadoop, and the algorithms are, in general, not R algorithms. Despite this, analytics with R have several issues related to large data. In order to analyze the dataset, R loads it into the memory, and if the dataset is large, it will fail with exceptions such as "cannot allocate vector of size x". Hence, in order to process large datasets, the processing power of R can be vastly magnified by combining it with the power of a Hadoop cluster. Hadoop is very a popular framework that provides such parallel processing capabilities. So, we can use R algorithms or analysis processing over Hadoop clusters to get the work done.

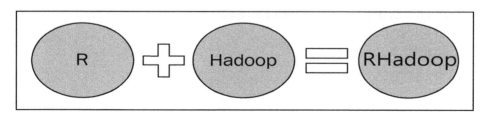

If we think about a combined RHadoop system, R will take care of data analysis operations with the preliminary functions, such as data loading, exploration, analysis, and visualization, and Hadoop will take care of parallel data storage as well as computation power against distributed data.

Prior to the advent of affordable Big Data technologies, analysis used to be run on limited datasets on a single machine. Advanced machine learning algorithms are very effective when applied to large datasets, and this is possible only with large clusters where data can be stored and processed with distributed data storage systems. In the next section, we will see how R and Hadoop can be installed on different operating systems and the possible ways to link R and Hadoop.

Installing R

You can download the appropriate version by visiting the official R website.

Here are the steps provided for three different operating systems. We have considered Windows, Linux, and Mac OS for R installation. Download the latest version of R as it will have all the latest patches and resolutions to the past bugs.

For Windows, follow the given steps:

1. Navigate to `www.r-project.org`.
2. Click on the **CRAN** section, select **CRAN mirror**, and select your Windows OS (stick to Linux; Hadoop is almost always used in a Linux environment).
3. Download the latest R version from the mirror.
4. Execute the downloaded `.exe` to install R.

For Linux-Ubuntu, follow the given steps:

1. Navigate to `www.r-project.org`.
2. Click on the **CRAN** section, select **CRAN mirror**, and select your OS.
3. In the `/etc/apt/sources.list` file, add the CRAN `<mirror>` entry.
4. Download and update the package lists from the repositories using the `sudo apt-get update` command.
5. Install R system using the `sudo apt-get install r-base` command.

For Linux-RHEL/CentOS, follow the given steps:

1. Navigate to `www.r-project.org`.
2. Click on **CRAN**, select **CRAN mirror**, and select Red Hat OS.
3. Download the `R-*core-*.rpm` file.
4. Install the `.rpm` package using the `rpm -ivh R-*core-*.rpm` command.
5. Install R system using `sudo yum install R`.

For Mac, follow the given steps:

1. Navigate to `www.r-project.org`.
2. Click on **CRAN**, select **CRAN mirror**, and select your OS.
3. Download the following files: `pkg`, `gfortran-*.dmg`, and `tcltk-*.dmg`.
4. Install the `R-*.pkg` file.
5. Then, install the `gfortran-*.dmg` and `tcltk-*.dmg` files.

After installing the base R package, it is advisable to install RStudio, which is a powerful and intuitive **Integrated Development Environment (IDE)** for R.

 We can use R distribution of Revolution Analytics as a Modern Data analytics tool for statistical computing and predictive analytics, which is available in free as well as premium versions. Hadoop integration is also available to perform Big Data analytics.

Installing RStudio

To install RStudio, perform the following steps:

1. Navigate to `http://www.rstudio.com/ide/download/desktop`.
2. Download the latest version of RStudio for your operating system.
3. Execute the installer file and install RStudio.

The RStudio organization and user community has developed a lot of R packages for graphics and visualization, such as `ggplot2`, `plyr`, `Shiny`, `Rpubs`, and `devtools`.

Understanding the features of R language

There are over 3,000 R packages and the list is growing day by day. It would be beyond the scope of any book to even attempt to explain all these packages. This book focuses only on the key features of R and the most frequently used and popular packages.

Using R packages

R packages are self-contained units of R functionality that can be invoked as functions. A good analogy would be a `.jar` file in Java. There is a vast library of R packages available for a very wide range of operations ranging from statistical operations and machine learning to rich graphic visualization and plotting. Every package will consist of one or more R functions. An R package is a re-usable entity that can be shared and used by others. R users can install the package that contains the functionality they are looking for and start calling the functions in the package. A comprehensive list of these packages can be found at `http://cran.r-project.org/` called **Comprehensive R Archive Network (CRAN)**.

Performing data operations

R enables a wide range of operations. Statistical operations, such as mean, min, max, probability, distribution, and regression. Machine learning operations, such as linear regression, logistic regression, classification, and clustering. Universal data processing operations are as follows:

- **Data cleaning**: This option is to clean massive datasets
- **Data exploration**: This option is to explore all the possible values of datasets
- **Data analysis**: This option is to perform analytics on data with descriptive and predictive analytics data visualization, that is, visualization of analysis output programming

To build an effective analytics application, sometimes we need to use the online **Application Programming Interface (API)** to dig up the data, analyze it with expedient services, and visualize it by third-party services. Also, to automate the data analysis process, programming will be the most useful feature to deal with.

R has its own programming language to operate data. Also, the available package can help to integrate R with other programming features. R supports object-oriented programming concepts. It is also capable of integrating with other programming languages, such as Java, PHP, C, and C++. There are several packages that will act as middle-layer programming features to aid in data analytics, which are similar to `sqldf`, `httr`, `RMongo`, `RgoogleMaps`, `RGoogleAnalytics`, and `google-prediction-api-r-client`.

Increasing community support

As the number of R users are escalating, the groups related to R are also increasing. So, R learners or developers can easily connect and get their uncertainty solved with the help of several R groups or communities.

The following are many popular sources that can be found useful:

- **R mailing list**: This is an official R group created by R project owners.
- **R blogs**: R has countless bloggers who are writing on several R applications. One of the most popular blog websites is `http://www.r-bloggers.com/` where all the bloggers contribute their blogs.
- **Stack overflow**: This is a great technical knowledge sharing platform where the programmers can post their technical queries and enthusiast programmers suggest a solution. For more information, visit `http://stats.stackexchange.com/`.
- **Groups**: There are many other groups existing on LinkedIn and Meetup where professionals across the world meet to discuss their problems and innovative ideas.
- **Books**: There are also lot of books about R. Some of the popular books are *R in Action,* by *Rob Kabacoff, Manning Publications, R in a Nutshell,* by *Joseph Adler, O'Reilly Media, R and Data Mining,* by *Yanchang Zhao, Academic Press,* and *R Graphs Cookbook,* by *Hrishi Mittal, Packt Publishing.*

Performing data modeling in R

Data modeling is a machine learning technique to identify the hidden pattern from the historical dataset, and this pattern will help in future value prediction over the same data. This techniques highly focus on past user actions and learns their taste. Most of these data modeling techniques have been adopted by many popular organizations to understand the behavior of their customers based on their past transactions. These techniques will analyze data and predict for the customers what they are looking for. Amazon, Google, Facebook, eBay, LinkedIn, Twitter, and many other organizations are using data mining for changing the definition applications.

The most common data mining techniques are as follows:

- **Regression**: In statistics, regression is a classic technique to identify the scalar relationship between two or more variables by fitting the state line on the variable values. That relationship will help to predict the variable value for future events. For example, any variable y can be modeled as linear function of another variable x with the formula $y = mx+c$. Here, x is the predictor variable, y is the response variable, m is slope of the line, and c is the intercept. Sales forecasting of products or services and predicting the price of stocks can be achieved through this regression. R provides this regression feature via the `lm` method, which is by default present in R.

- **Classification**: This is a machine-learning technique used for labeling the set of observations provided for training examples. With this, we can classify the observations into one or more labels. The likelihood of sales, online fraud detection, and cancer classification (for medical science) are common applications of classification problems. Google Mail uses this technique to classify e-mails as spam or not. Classification features can be served by `glm`, `glmnet`, `ksvm`, `svm`, and `randomForest` in R.

- **Clustering**: This technique is all about organizing similar items into groups from the given collection of items. User segmentation and image compression are the most common applications of clustering. Market segmentation, social network analysis, organizing the computer clustering, and astronomical data analysis are applications of clustering. Google News uses these techniques to group similar news items into the same category. Clustering can be achieved through the `knn`, `kmeans`, `dist`, `pvclust`, and `Mclust` methods in R.

- **Recommendation**: The recommendation algorithms are used in recommender systems where these systems are the most immediately recognizable machine learning techniques in use today. Web content recommendations may include similar websites, blogs, videos, or related content. Also, recommendation of online items can be helpful for cross-selling and up-selling. We have all seen online shopping portals that attempt to recommend books, mobiles, or any items that can be sold on the Web based on the user's past behavior. Amazon is a well-known e-commerce portal that generates 29 percent of sales through recommendation systems. Recommender systems can be implemented via `Recommender()` with the `recommenderlab` package in R.

Installing Hadoop

Now, we presume that you are aware of R, what it is, how to install it, what it's key features are, and why you may want to use it. Now we need to know the limitations of R (this is a better introduction to Hadoop). Before processing the data; R needs to load the data into **random access memory (RAM)**. So, the data needs to be smaller than the available machine memory. For data that is larger than the machine memory, we consider it as Big Data (only in our case as there are many other definitions of Big Data).

To avoid this Big Data issue, we need to scale the hardware configuration; however, this is a temporary solution. To get this solved, we need to get a Hadoop cluster that is able to store it and perform parallel computation across a large computer cluster. Hadoop is the most popular solution. Hadoop is an open source Java framework, which is the top level project handled by the Apache software foundation. Hadoop is inspired by the Google filesystem and MapReduce, mainly designed for operating on Big Data by distributed processing.

Hadoop mainly supports Linux operating systems. To run this on Windows, we need to use VMware to host Ubuntu within the Windows OS. There are many ways to use and install Hadoop, but here we will consider the way that supports R best. Before we combine R and Hadoop, let us understand what Hadoop is.

> Machine learning contains all the data modeling techniques that can be explored with the web link `http://en.wikipedia.org/wiki/Machine_learning`.
>
> The structure blog on Hadoop installation by Michael Noll can be found at `http://www.michael-noll.com/tutorials/running-hadoop-on-ubuntu-linux-single-node-cluster/`.

Understanding different Hadoop modes

Hadoop is used with three different modes:

- **The standalone mode**: In this mode, you do not need to start any Hadoop daemons. Instead, just call ~/Hadoop-directory/bin/hadoop that will execute a Hadoop operation as a single Java process. This is recommended for testing purposes. This is the default mode and you don't need to configure anything else. All daemons, such as NameNode, DataNode, JobTracker, and TaskTracker run in a single Java process.

- **The pseudo mode**: In this mode, you configure Hadoop for all the nodes. A separate **Java Virtual Machine (JVM)** is spawned for each of the Hadoop components or daemons like mini cluster on a single host.

- **The full distributed mode**: In this mode, Hadoop is distributed across multiple machines. Dedicated hosts are configured for Hadoop components. Therefore, separate JVM processes are present for all daemons.

Understanding Hadoop installation steps

Hadoop can be installed in several ways; we will consider the way that is better to integrate with R. We will choose Ubuntu OS as it is easy to install and access it.

1. Installing Hadoop on Linux, Ubuntu flavor (single and multinode cluster).
2. Installing Cloudera Hadoop on Ubuntu.

Installing Hadoop on Linux, Ubuntu flavor (single node cluster)

To install Hadoop over Ubuntu OS with the pseudo mode, we need to meet the following prerequisites:

- Sun Java 6
- Dedicated Hadoop system user
- Configuring SSH
- Disabling IPv6

 The provided Hadoop installation will be supported with Hadoop MRv1.

Follow the given steps to install Hadoop:

1. Download the latest Hadoop sources from the Apache software foundation. Here we have considered Apache Hadoop 1.0.3, whereas the latest version is 1.1.x.

```
// Locate to Hadoop installation directory
$ cd /usr/local

// Extract the tar file of Hadoop distribution
$ sudo tar xzf hadoop-1.0.3.tar.gz

// To move Hadoop resources to hadoop folder
$ sudo mv hadoop-1.0.3 hadoop

// Make user-hduser from group-hadoop as owner of hadoop directory
$ sudo chown -R hduser:hadoop hadoop
```

2. Add the $JAVA_HOME and $HADOOP_HOME variables to the .bashrc file of Hadoop system user and the updated .bashrc file looks as follows:

```
// Setting the environment variables for running Java and Hadoop
commands
export HADOOP_HOME=/usr/local/hadoop
export JAVA_HOME=/usr/lib/jvm/java-6-sun

// alias for Hadoop commands
unalias fs &> /dev/null
alias fs="hadoop fs"
unalias hls &> /dev/null
aliashls="fs -ls"

// Defining the function for compressing the MapReduce job output
by lzop command
lzohead () {
hadoopfs -cat $1 | lzop -dc | head -1000 | less
}

// Adding Hadoop_HoME variable to PATH
export PATH=$PATH:$HADOOP_HOME/bin
```

3. Update the Hadoop configuration files with the conf/*-site.xml format.

Finally, the three files will look as follows:

- conf/core-site.xml:

```
<property>
<name>hadoop.tmp.dir</name>
<value>/app/hadoop/tmp</value>
<description>A base for other temporary directories.</description>
</property>
<property>
<name>fs.default.name</name>
<value>hdfs://localhost:54310</value>
<description>The name of the default filesystem. A URI whose
scheme and authority determine the FileSystem implementation. The
uri's scheme determines the config property (fs.SCHEME.impl)
naming
theFileSystem implementation class. The uri's authority is used to
determine the host, port, etc. for a filesystem.</description>
</property>
```

- conf/mapred-site.xml:

```
<property>
<name>mapred.job.tracker</name>
<value>localhost:54311</value>
<description>The host and port that the MapReduce job tracker runs
at. If "local", then jobs are run in-process as a single map
and reduce task.
</description>
</property>
```

- conf/hdfs-site.xml:

```
<property>
<name>dfs.replication</name>
<value>1</value>
<description>Default block replication.
  The actual number of replications can be specified when the file
is created.
  The default is used if replication is not specified in create
time.
</description>
```

After completing the editing of these configuration files, we need to set up the distributed filesystem across the Hadoop clusters or node.

- Format **Hadoop Distributed File System (HDFS)** via NameNode by using the following command line:

```
hduser@ubuntu:~$ /usr/local/hadoop/bin/hadoopnamenode -format
```

- Start your single node cluster by using the following command line:

```
hduser@ubuntu:~$ /usr/local/hadoop/bin/start-all.sh
```

> **Downloading the example code**
>
> You can download the example code files for all Packt books you have purchased from your account at http://www.packtpub.com. If you purchased this book elsewhere, you can visit http://www.packtpub.com/support and register to have the files e-mailed directly to you.

Installing Hadoop on Linux, Ubuntu flavor (multinode cluster)

We learned how to install Hadoop on a single node cluster. Now we will see how to install Hadoop on a multinode cluster (the full distributed mode).

For this, we need several nodes configured with a single node Hadoop cluster. To install Hadoop on multinodes, we need to have that machine configured with a single node Hadoop cluster as described in the last section.

After getting the single node Hadoop cluster installed, we need to perform the following steps:

1. In the networking phase, we are going to use two nodes for setting up a full distributed Hadoop mode. To communicate with each other, the nodes need to be in the same network in terms of software and hardware configuration.

2. Among these two, one of the nodes will be considered as master and the other will be considered as slave. So, for performing Hadoop operations, master needs to be connected to slave. We will enter 192.168.0.1 in the master machine and 192.168.0.2 in the slave machine.

3. Update the /etc/hosts directory in both the nodes. It will look as 192.168.0.1 master and 192.168.0.2 slave.

You can perform the **Secure Shell (SSH)** setup similar to what we did for a single node cluster setup. For more details, visit `http://www.michael-noll.com`.

4. Updating `conf/*-site.xml`: We must change all these configuration files in all of the nodes.

    ○ `conf/core-site.xml` and `conf/mapred-site.xml`: In the single node setup, we have updated these files. So, now we need to just replace `localhost` by `master` in the value tag.

    ○ `conf/hdfs-site.xml`: In the single node setup, we have set the value of `dfs.replication` as 1. Now we need to update this as 2.

5. In the formatting HDFS phase, before we start the multinode cluster, we need to format HDFS with the following command (from the master node):

    ```
    bin/hadoop namenode -format
    ```

Now, we have completed all the steps to install the multinode Hadoop cluster. To start the Hadoop clusters, we need to follow these steps:

1. Start HDFS daemons:

    ```
    hduser@master:/usr/local/hadoop$ bin/start-dfs.sh
    ```

2. Start MapReduce daemons:

    ```
    hduser@master:/usr/local/hadoop$ bin/start-mapred.sh
    ```

3. Alternatively, we can start all the daemons with a single command:

    ```
    hduser@master:/usr/local/hadoop$ bin/start-all.sh
    ```

4. To stop all these daemons, fire:

    ```
    hduser@master:/usr/local/hadoop$ bin/stop-all.sh
    ```

These installation steps are reproduced after being inspired by the blogs (`http://www.michael-noll.com`) of Michael Noll, who is a researcher and Software Engineer based in Switzerland, Europe. He works as a Technical lead for a large scale computing infrastructure on the Apache Hadoop stack at VeriSign.

Now the Hadoop cluster has been set up on your machines. For the installation of the same Hadoop cluster on single node or multinode with extended Hadoop components, try the Cloudera tool.

Installing Cloudera Hadoop on Ubuntu

Cloudera Hadoop (CDH) is Cloudera's open source distribution that targets enterprise class deployments of Hadoop technology. Cloudera is also a sponsor of the Apache software foundation. CDH is available in two versions: CDH3 and CDH4. To install one of these, you must have Ubuntu with either 10.04 LTS or 12.04 LTS (also, you can try CentOS, Debian, and Red Hat systems). Cloudera manager will make this installation easier for you if you are installing a Hadoop on cluster of computers, which provides GUI-based Hadoop and its component installation over a whole cluster. This tool is very much recommended for large clusters.

We need to meet the following prerequisites:

- Configuring SSH
- OS with the following criteria:
    - Ubuntu 10.04 LTS or 12.04 LTS with 64 bit
    - Red Hat Enterprise Linux 5 or 6
    - CentOS 5 or 6
    - Oracle Enterprise Linux 5
    - SUSE Linux Enterprise server 11 (SP1 or lasso)
    - Debian 6.0

The installation steps are as follows:

1. Download and run the Cloudera manager installer: To initialize the Cloudera manager installation process, we need to first download the `cloudera-manager-installer.bin` file from the download section of the Cloudera website. After that, store it at the cluster so that all the nodes can access this. Allow ownership for execution permission of `cloudera-manager-installer.bin` to the user. Run the following command to start execution.

   ```
   $ sudo ./cloudera-manager-installer.bin
   ```

2. Read the Cloudera manager **Readme** and then click on **Next**.

3. Start the Cloudera manager admin console: The Cloudera manager admin console allows you to use Cloudera manager to install, manage, and monitor Hadoop on your cluster. After accepting the license from the Cloudera service provider, you need to traverse to your local web browser by entering `http://localhost:7180` in your address bar. You can also use any of the following browsers:
    - Firefox 11 or higher
    - Google Chrome
    - Internet Explorer
    - Safari

4. Log in to the Cloudera manager console with the default credentials using `admin` for both the username and password. Later on you can change it as per your choice.

5. Use the Cloudera manager for automated CDH3 installation and configuration via browser: This step will install most of the required Cloudera Hadoop packages from Cloudera to your machines. The steps are as follows:

   1. Install and validate your Cloudera manager license key file if you have chosen a full version of software.

   2. Specify the hostname or IP address range for your CDH cluster installation.

   3. Connect to each host with SSH.

   4. Install the **Java Development Kit (JDK)** (if not already installed), the Cloudera manager agent, and CDH3 or CDH4 on each cluster host.

   5. Configure Hadoop on each node and start the Hadoop services.

6. After running the wizard and using the Cloudera manager, you should change the default administrator password as soon as possible. To change the administrator password, follow these steps:

   1. Click on the icon with the gear sign to display the administration page.

   2. Open the **Password** tab.

   3. Enter a new password twice and then click on **Update**.

7. Test the Cloudera Hadoop installation: You can check the Cloudera manager installation on your cluster by logging into the Cloudera manager admin console and by clicking on the **Services** tab. You should see something like the following screenshot:

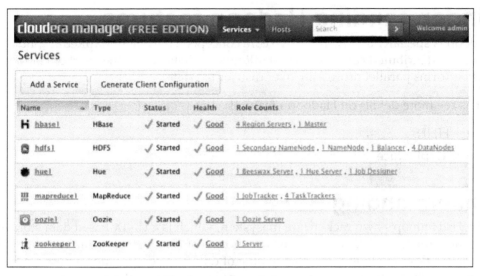

Cloudera manager admin console

8. You can also click on each service to see more detailed information. For example, if you click on the **hdfs1** link, you might see something like the following screenshot:

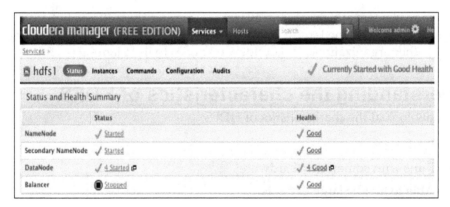

Cloudera manger admin console – HDFS service

To avoid these installation steps, use preconfigured Hadoop instances with Amazon Elastic MapReduce and MapReduce.

If you want to use Hadoop on Windows, try the HDP tool by Hortonworks. This is 100 percent open source, enterprise grade distribution of Hadoop. You can download the HDP tool at http://hortonworks.com/download/.

Understanding Hadoop features

Hadoop is specially designed for two core concepts: HDFS and MapReduce. Both are related to distributed computation. MapReduce is believed as the heart of Hadoop that performs parallel processing over distributed data.

Let us see more details on Hadoop's features:

- HDFS
- MapReduce

Understanding HDFS

HDFS is Hadoop's own rack-aware filesystem, which is a UNIX-based data storage layer of Hadoop. HDFS is derived from concepts of Google filesystem. An important characteristic of Hadoop is the partitioning of data and computation across many (thousands of) hosts, and the execution of application computations in parallel, close to their data. On HDFS, data files are replicated as sequences of blocks in the cluster. A Hadoop cluster scales computation capacity, storage capacity, and I/O bandwidth by simply adding commodity servers. HDFS can be accessed from applications in many different ways. Natively, HDFS provides a Java API for applications to use.

The Hadoop clusters at Yahoo! span 40,000 servers and store 40 petabytes of application data, with the largest Hadoop cluster being 4,000 servers. Also, one hundred other organizations worldwide are known to use Hadoop.

Understanding the characteristics of HDFS

Let us now look at the characteristics of HDFS:

- Fault tolerant
- Runs with commodity hardware
- Able to handle large datasets
- Master slave paradigm
- Write once file access only

Understanding MapReduce

MapReduce is a programming model for processing large datasets distributed on a large cluster. MapReduce is the heart of Hadoop. Its programming paradigm allows performing massive data processing across thousands of servers configured with Hadoop clusters. This is derived from Google MapReduce.

Hadoop MapReduce is a software framework for writing applications easily, which process large amounts of data (multiterabyte datasets) in parallel on large clusters (thousands of nodes) of commodity hardware in a reliable, fault-tolerant manner. This MapReduce paradigm is divided into two phases, Map and Reduce that mainly deal with key and value pairs of data. The Map and Reduce task run sequentially in a cluster; the output of the Map phase becomes the input for the Reduce phase. These phases are explained as follows:

- **Map phase**: Once divided, datasets are assigned to the task tracker to perform the Map phase. The data functional operation will be performed over the data, emitting the mapped key and value pairs as the output of the Map phase.

- **Reduce phase**: The master node then collects the answers to all the subproblems and combines them in some way to form the output; the answer to the problem it was originally trying to solve.

The five common steps of parallel computing are as follows:

1. Preparing the Map() input: This will take the input data row wise and emit key value pairs per rows, or we can explicitly change as per the requirement.
   - Map input: list (k1, v1)

2. Run the user-provided Map() code
   - Map output: list (k2, v2)

3. Shuffle the Map output to the Reduce processors. Also, shuffle the similar keys (grouping them) and input them to the same reducer.

4. Run the user-provided Reduce() code: This phase will run the custom reducer code designed by developer to run on shuffled data and emit key and value.
   - Reduce input: (k2, list(v2))
   - Reduce output: (k3, v3)

5. Produce the final output: Finally, the master node collects all reducer output and combines and writes them in a text file.

 The reference links to review on Google filesystem can be found at http://research.google.com/archive/gfs.html and

Google MapReduce can be found at http://research.google.com/archive/mapreduce.html.

Learning the HDFS and MapReduce architecture

Since HDFS and MapReduce are considered to be the two main features of the Hadoop framework, we will focus on them. So, let's first start with HDFS.

Understanding the HDFS architecture

HDFS can be presented as the master/slave architecture. HDFS master is named as NameNode whereas slave as DataNode. NameNode is a sever that manages the filesystem namespace and adjusts the access (open, close, rename, and more) to files by the client. It divides the input data into blocks and announces which data block will be store in which DataNode. DataNode is a slave machine that stores the replicas of the partitioned dataset and serves the data as the request comes. It also performs block creation and deletion.

The internal mechanism of HDFS divides the file into one or more blocks; these blocks are stored in a set of data nodes. Under normal circumstances of the replication factor three, the HDFS strategy is to place the first copy on the local node, second copy on the local rack with a different node, and a third copy into different racks with different nodes. As HDFS is designed to support large files, the HDFS block size is defined as 64 MB. If required, this can be increased.

Understanding HDFS components

HDFS is managed with the master-slave architecture included with the following components:

- **NameNode**: This is the master of the HDFS system. It maintains the directories, files, and manages the blocks that are present on the DataNodes.

- **DataNode**: These are slaves that are deployed on each machine and provide actual storage. They are responsible for serving read-and-write data requests for the clients.

- **Secondary NameNode**: This is responsible for performing periodic checkpoints. So, if the NameNode fails at any time, it can be replaced with a snapshot image stored by the secondary NameNode checkpoints.

Understanding the MapReduce architecture

MapReduce is also implemented over master-slave architectures. Classic MapReduce contains job submission, job initialization, task assignment, task execution, progress and status update, and job completion-related activities, which are mainly managed by the JobTracker node and executed by TaskTracker. Client application submits a job to the JobTracker. Then input is divided across the cluster. The JobTracker then calculates the number of map and reducer to be processed. It commands the TaskTracker to start executing the job. Now, the TaskTracker copies the resources to a local machine and launches JVM to map and reduce program over the data. Along with this, the TaskTracker periodically sends update to the JobTracker, which can be considered as the heartbeat that helps to update JobID, job status, and usage of resources.

Understanding MapReduce components

MapReduce is managed with master-slave architecture included with the following components:

- **JobTracker**: This is the master node of the MapReduce system, which manages the jobs and resources in the cluster (TaskTrackers). The JobTracker tries to schedule each map as close to the actual data being processed on the TaskTracker, which is running on the same DataNode as the underlying block.
- **TaskTracker**: These are the slaves that are deployed on each machine. They are responsible for running the map and reducing tasks as instructed by the JobTracker.

Understanding the HDFS and MapReduce architecture by plot

In this plot, both HDFS and MapReduce master and slave components have been included, where NameNode and DataNode are from HDFS and JobTracker and TaskTracker are from the MapReduce paradigm.

Both paradigms consisting of master and slave candidates have their own specific responsibility to handle MapReduce and HDFS operations. In the next plot, there is a plot with two sections: the preceding one is a MapReduce layer and the following one is an HDFS layer.

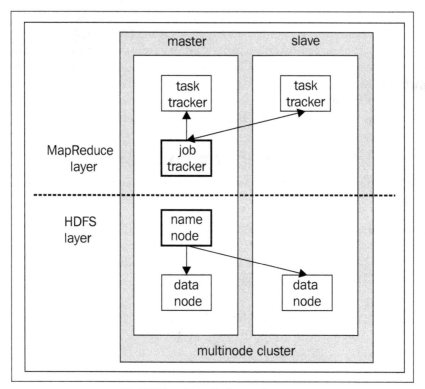

The HDFS and MapReduce architecture

Hadoop is a top-level Apache project and is a very complicated Java framework. To avoid technical complications, the Hadoop community has developed a number of Java frameworks that has added an extra value to Hadoop features. They are considered as Hadoop subprojects. Here, we are departing to discuss several Hadoop components that can be considered as an abstraction of HDFS or MapReduce.

Understanding Hadoop subprojects

Mahout is a popular data mining library. It takes the most popular data mining scalable machine learning algorithms for performing clustering, classification, regression, and statistical modeling to prepare intelligent applications. Also, it is a scalable machine-learning library.

Apache Mahout is distributed under a commercially friendly Apache software license. The goal of Apache Mahout is to build a vibrant, responsive, and diverse community to facilitate discussions not only on the project itself but also on potential use cases.

The following are some companies that are using Mahout:

- **Amazon**: This a shopping portal for providing personalization recommendation
- **AOL**: This is a shopping portal for shopping recommendations
- **Drupal**: This is a PHP content management system using Mahout for providing open source content-based recommendation
- **iOffer**: This is a shopping portal, which uses Mahout's Frequent Pattern Set Mining and collaborative filtering to recommend items to users
- **LucidWorks Big Data**: This is a popular analytics firm, which uses Mahout for clustering, duplicate document detection, phase extraction, and classification
- **Radoop**: This provides a drag-and-drop interface for Big Data analytics, including Mahout clustering and classification algorithms
- **Twitter**: This is a social networking site, which uses Mahout's **Latent Dirichlet Allocation (LDA)** implementation for user interest modeling and maintains a fork of Mahout on GitHub.
- **Yahoo!**: This is the world's most popular web service provider, which uses Mahout's Frequent Pattern Set Mining for Yahoo! Mail

 The reference links on the Hadoop ecosystem can be found at `http://www.revelytix.com/?q=content/hadoop-ecosystem`.

Apache HBase is a distributed Big Data store for Hadoop. This allows random, real-time read/write access to Big Data. This is designed as a column-oriented data storage model innovated after inspired by Google BigTable.

The following are the companies using HBase:

- **Yahoo!**: This is the world's popular web service provider for near duplicate document detection
- **Twitter**: This is a social networking site for version control storage and retrieval
- **Mahalo**: This is a knowledge sharing service for similar content recommendation
- **NING**: This is a social network service provider for real-time analytics and reporting
- **StumbleUpon**: This is a universal personalized recommender system, real-time data storage, and data analytics platform
- **Veoh**: This is an online multimedia content sharing platform for user profiling system

 For Google Big Data, distributed storage system for structured data, refer the link `http://research.google.com/archive/bigtable.html`.

Hive is a Hadoop-based data warehousing like framework developed by Facebook. It allows users to fire queries in SQL-like languages, such as HiveQL, which are highly abstracted to Hadoop MapReduce. This allows SQL programmers with no MapReduce experience to use the warehouse and makes it easier to integrate with business intelligence and visualization tools for real-time query processing.

Pig is a Hadoop-based open source platform for analyzing the large scale datasets via its own SQL-like language: Pig Latin. This provides a simple operation and programming interface for massive, complex data-parallelization computation. This is also easier to develop; it's more optimized and extensible. Apache Pig has been developed by Yahoo!. Currently, Yahoo! and Twitter are the primary Pig users.

For developers, the direct use of Java APIs can be tedious or error-prone, but also limits the Java programmer's use of Hadoop programming's flexibility. So, Hadoop provides two solutions that enable making Hadoop programming for dataset management and dataset analysis with MapReduce easier — these are Pig and Hive, which are always confusing.

Apache Sqoop provides Hadoop data processing platform and relational databases, data warehouse, and other non-relational databases quickly transferring large amounts of data in a new way. Apache Sqoop is a mutual data tool for importing data from the relational databases to Hadoop HDFS and exporting data from HDFS to relational databases.

It works together with most modern relational databases, such as MySQL, PostgreSQL, Oracle, Microsoft SQL Server, and IBM DB2, and enterprise data warehouse. Sqoop extension API provides a way to create new connectors for the database system. Also, the Sqoop source comes up with some popular database connectors. To perform this operation, Sqoop first transforms the data into Hadoop MapReduce with some logic of database schema creation and transformation.

Apache Zookeeper is also a Hadoop subproject used for managing Hadoop, Hive, Pig, HBase, Solr, and other projects. Zookeeper is an open source distributed applications coordination service, which is designed with Fast Paxos algorithm-based synchronization and configuration and naming services such as maintenance of distributed applications. In programming, Zookeeper design is a very simple data model style, much like the system directory tree structure.

Zookeeper is divided into two parts: the server and client. For a cluster of Zookeeper servers, only one acts as a leader, which accepts and coordinates all rights. The rest of the servers are read-only copies of the master. If the leader server goes down, any other server can start serving all requests. Zookeeper clients are connected to a server on the Zookeeper service. The client sends a request, receives a response, accesses the observer events, and sends a heartbeat via a TCP connection with the server.

For a high-performance coordination service for distributed applications, Zookeeper is a centralized service for maintaining configuration information, naming, and providing distributed synchronization and group services. All these kinds of services are used in some form or another by distributed applications. Each time they are implemented, there is a lot of work that goes into fixing the bugs and race conditions that are inevitable. These services lead to management complexity when the applications are deployed.

Apache Solr is an open source enterprise search platform from the Apache license project. Apache Solr is highly scalable, supporting distributed search and index replication engine. This allows building web application with powerful text search, faceted search, real-time indexing, dynamic clustering, database integration, and rich document handling.

Apache Solr is written in Java, which runs as a standalone server to serve the search results via REST-like HTTP/XML and JSON APIs. So, this Solr server can be easily integrated with an application, which is written in other programming languages. Due to all these features, this search server is used by Netflix, AOL, CNET, and Zappos.

Ambari is very specific to Hortonworks. Apache Ambari is a web-based tool that supports Apache Hadoop cluster supply, management, and monitoring. Ambari handles most of the Hadoop components, including HDFS, MapReduce, Hive, Pig, HBase, Zookeeper, Sqoop, and HCatlog as centralized management.

In addition, Ambari is able to install security based on the Kerberos authentication protocol over the Hadoop cluster. Also, it provides role-based user authentication, authorization, and auditing functions for users to manage integrated LDAP and Active Directory.

Summary

In this chapter, we learned what is R, Hadoop, and their features, and how to install them before going on to analyzing the datasets with R and Hadoop. In the next chapter, we are going to learn what MapReduce is and how to develop MapReduce programs with Apache Hadoop.

2
Writing Hadoop MapReduce Programs

In the previous chapter, we learned how to set up the R and Hadoop development environment. Since we are interested in performing Big Data analytics, we need to learn Hadoop to perform operations with Hadoop MapReduce. In this chapter, we will discuss what MapReduce is, why it is necessary, how MapReduce programs can be developed through Apache Hadoop, and more.

In this chapter, we will cover:

- Understanding the basics of MapReduce
- Introducing Hadoop MapReduce
- Understanding the Hadoop MapReduce fundamentals
- Writing a Hadoop MapReduce example
- Understanding several possible MapReduce definitions to solve business problems
- Learning different ways to write Hadoop MapReduce in R

Understanding the basics of MapReduce

Understanding the basics of MapReduce could well be a long-term solution if one doesn't have a cluster or uses **Message Passing Interface** (**MPI**). However, a more realistic use case is when the data doesn't fit on one disk but fits on a **Distributed File System** (**DFS**), or already lives on Hadoop-related software.

Moreover, MapReduce is a programming model that works in a distributed fashion, but it is not the only one that does. It might be illuminating to describe other programming models, for example, MPI and **Bulk Synchronous Parallel (BSP)**. To process Big Data with tools such as R and several machine learning techniques requires a high-configuration machine, but that's not the permanent solution. So, distributed processing is the key to handling this data. This distributed computation can be implemented with the MapReduce programming model.

MapReduce is the one that answers the Big Data question. Logically, to process data we need parallel processing, which means processing over large computation; it can either be obtained by clustering the computers or increasing the configuration of the machine. Using the computer cluster is an ideal way to process data with a large size.

Before we talk more about MapReduce by parallel processing, we will discuss Google MapReduce research and a white paper written by *Jeffrey Dean* and *Sanjay Ghemawat* in 2004. They introduced MapReduce as simplified data processing software on large clusters. MapReduce implementation runs on large clusters with commodity hardware. This data processing platform is easier for programmers to perform various operations. The system takes care of input data, distributes data across the computer network, processes it in parallel, and finally combines its output into a single file to be aggregated later. This is very helpful in terms of cost and is also a time-saving system for processing large datasets over the cluster. Also, it will efficiently use computer resources to perform analytics over huge data. Google has been granted a patent on MapReduce.

For MapReduce, programmers need to just design/migrate applications into two phases: Map and Reduce. They simply have to design Map functions for processing a key-value pair to generate a set of intermediate key-value pairs, and Reduce functions to merge all the intermediate keys. Both the Map and Reduce functions maintain MapReduce workflow. The Reduce function will start executing the code after completion or once the Map output is available to it.

Their execution sequence can be seen as follows:

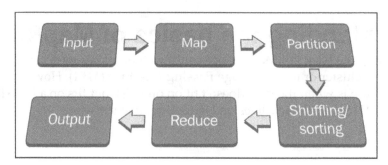

MapReduce assumes that the Maps are independent and will execute them in parallel. The key aspect of the MapReduce algorithm is that if every Map and Reduce is independent of all other ongoing Maps and Reduces in the network, the operation will run in parallel on different keys and lists of data.

A distributed filesystem spreads multiple copies of data across different machines. This offers reliability as well as fault tolerance. If a machine with one copy of the file crashes, the same data will be provided from another replicated data source.

The master node of the MapReduce daemon will take care of all the responsibilities of the MapReduce jobs, such as the execution of jobs, the scheduling of Mappers, Reducers, Combiners, and Partitioners, the monitoring of successes as well as failures of individual job tasks, and finally, the completion of the batch job.

Apache Hadoop processes the distributed data in a parallel manner by running Hadoop MapReduce jobs on servers near the data stored on Hadoop's distributed filesystem.

Companies using MapReduce include:

- **Amazon**: This is an online e-commerce and cloud web service provider for Big Data analytics
- **eBay**: This is an e-commerce portal for finding articles by its description
- **Google**: This is a web search engine for finding relevant pages relating to a particular topic
- **LinkedIn**: This is a professional networking site for Big Data storage and generating personalized recommendations
- **Trovit**: This is a vertical search engine for finding jobs that match a given description
- **Twitter**: This is a social networking site for finding messages

Apart from these, there are many other brands that are using Hadoop for Big Data analytics.

Introducing Hadoop MapReduce

Basically, the MapReduce model can be implemented in several languages, but apart from that, Hadoop MapReduce is a popular Java framework for easily written applications. It processes vast amounts of data (multiterabyte datasets) in parallel on large clusters (thousands of nodes) of commodity hardware in a reliable and fault-tolerant manner. This MapReduce paradigm is divided into two phases, Map and Reduce, that mainly deal with key-value pairs of data. The Map and Reduce tasks run sequentially in a cluster, and the output of the Map phase becomes the input of the Reduce phase.

All data input elements in MapReduce cannot be updated. If the input (key, value) pairs for mapping tasks are changed, it will not be reflected in the input files. The Mapper output will be piped to the appropriate Reducer grouped with the key attribute as input. This sequential data process will be carried away in a parallel manner with the help of Hadoop MapReduce algorithms as well as Hadoop clusters.

MapReduce programs transform the input dataset present in the list format into output data that will also be in the list format. This logical list translation process is mostly repeated twice in the Map and Reduce phases. We can also handle these repetitions by fixing the number of Mappers and Reducers. In the next section, MapReduce concepts are described based on the old MapReduce API.

Listing Hadoop MapReduce entities

The following are the components of Hadoop that are responsible for performing analytics over Big Data:

- **Client**: This initializes the job
- **JobTracker**: This monitors the job
- **TaskTracker**: This executes the job
- **HDFS**: This stores the input and output data

Understanding the Hadoop MapReduce scenario

The four main stages of Hadoop MapReduce data processing are as follows:

- The loading of data into HDFS
- The execution of the Map phase
- Shuffling and sorting
- The execution of the Reduce phase

Loading data into HDFS

The input dataset needs to be uploaded to the Hadoop directory so it can be used by MapReduce nodes. Then, **Hadoop Distributed File System (HDFS)** will divide the input dataset into data splits and store them to DataNodes in a cluster by taking care of the replication factor for fault tolerance. All the data splits will be processed by TaskTracker for the Map and Reduce tasks in a parallel manner.

Also, there are some alternative ways to get the dataset in HDFS with Hadoop components:

- **Sqoop**: This is an open source tool designed for efficiently transferring bulk data between Apache Hadoop and structured, relational databases. Suppose your application has already been configured with the MySQL database and you want to use the same data for performing data analytics, Sqoop is recommended for importing datasets to HDFS. Also, after the completion of the data analytics process, the output can be exported to the MySQL database.

- **Flume**: This is a distributed, reliable, and available service for efficiently collecting, aggregating, and moving large amounts of log data to HDFS. Flume is able to read data from most sources, such as logfiles, sys logs, and the standard output of the Unix process.

Using the preceding data collection and moving the framework can make this data transfer process very easy for the MapReduce application for data analytics.

Executing the Map phase

Executing the client application starts the Hadoop MapReduce processes. The Map phase then copies the job resources (unjarred class files) and stores it to HDFS, and requests JobTracker to execute the job. The JobTracker initializes the job, retrieves the input, splits the information, and creates a Map task for each job.

The JobTracker will call TaskTracker to run the Map task over the assigned input data subset. The Map task reads this input split data as input (`key`, `value`) pairs provided to the Mapper method, which then produces intermediate (`key`, `value`) pairs. There will be at least one output for each input (`key`, `value`) pair.

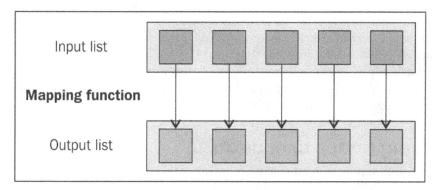

Mapping individual elements of an input list

The list of (key, value) pairs is generated such that the key attribute will be repeated many times. So, its key attribute will be re-used in the Reducer for aggregating values in MapReduce. As far as format is concerned, Mapper output format values and Reducer input values must be the same.

After the completion of this Map operation, the TaskTracker will keep the result in its buffer storage and local disk space (if the output data size is more than the threshold).

For example, suppose we have a Map function that converts the input text into lowercase. This will convert the list of input strings into a list of lowercase strings.

> **Keys and values**: In MapReduce, every value has its identifier that is considered as key. The key-value pairs received by the Mapper are dependent on the input datatype as specified in the job configuration file.

Shuffling and sorting

To optimize the MapReduce program, this intermediate phase is very important.

As soon as the Mapper output from the Map phase is available, this intermediate phase will be called automatically. After the completion of the Map phase, all the emitted intermediate (key, value) pairs will be partitioned by a Partitioner at the Mapper side, only if the Partitioner is present. The output of the Partitioner will be sorted out based on the key attribute at the Mapper side. Output from sorting the operation is stored on buffer memory available at the Mapper node, TaskTracker.

The Combiner is often the Reducer itself. So by compression, it's not **Gzip** or some similar compression but the Reducer on the node that the map is outputting the data on. The data returned by the Combiner is then shuffled and sent to the reduced nodes. To speed up data transmission of the Mapper output to the Reducer slot at TaskTracker, you need to compress that output with the Combiner function. By default, the Mapper output will be stored to buffer memory, and if the output size is larger than threshold, it will be stored to a local disk. This output data will be available through **Hypertext Transfer Protocol (HTTP)**.

Reducing phase execution

As soon as the Mapper output is available, TaskTracker in the Reducer node will retrieve the available partitioned Map's output data, and they will be grouped together and merged into one large file, which will then be assigned to a process with a Reducer method. Finally, this will be sorted out before data is provided to the Reducer method.

The `Reducer` method receives a list of input values from an input (`key`, `list (value)`) and aggregates them based on custom logic, and produces the output (`key`, `value`) pairs.

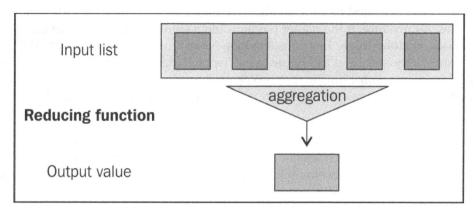

Reducing input values to an aggregate value as output

The output of the `Reducer` method of the Reduce phase will directly be written into HDFS as per the format specified by the MapReduce job configuration class.

Understanding the limitations of MapReduce

Let's see some of Hadoop MapReduce's limitations:

- The MapReduce framework is notoriously difficult to leverage for transformational logic that is not as simple, for example, real-time streaming, graph processing, and message passing.
- Data querying is inefficient over distributed, unindexed data than in a database created with indexed data. However, if the index over the data is generated, it needs to be maintained when the data is removed or added.
- We can't parallelize the Reduce task to the Map task to reduce the overall processing time because Reduce tasks do not start until the output of the Map tasks is available to it. (The Reducer's input is fully dependent on the Mapper's output.) Also, we can't control the sequence of the execution of the Map and Reduce task. But sometimes, based on application logic, we can definitely configure a slow start for the Reduce tasks at the instance when the data collection starts as soon as the Map tasks complete.
- Long-running Reduce tasks can't be completed because of their poor resource utilization either if the Reduce task is taking too much time to complete and fails or if there are no other Reduce slots available for rescheduling it (this can be solved with YARN).

Understanding Hadoop's ability to solve problems

Since this book is geared towards analysts, it might be relevant to provide analytical examples; for instance, if the reader has a problem similar to the one described previously, Hadoop might be of use. Hadoop is not a universal solution to all Big Data issues; it's just a good technique to use when large data needs to be divided into small chunks and distributed across servers that need to be processed in a parallel fashion. This saves time and the cost of performing analytics over a huge dataset.

If we are able to design the Map and Reduce phase for the problem, it will be possible to solve it with MapReduce. Generally, Hadoop provides computation power to process data that does not fit into machine memory. (R users mostly found an error message while processing large data and see the following message: cannot allocate vector of size 2.5 GB.)

Understanding the different Java concepts used in Hadoop programming

There are some classic Java concepts that make Hadoop more interactive. They are as follows:

- **Remote procedure calls**: This is an interprocess communication that allows a computer program to cause a subroutine or procedure to execute in another address space (commonly on another computer on shared network) without the programmer explicitly coding the details for this remote interaction. That is, the programmer writes essentially the same code whether the subroutine is local to the executing program or remote.

- **Serialization/Deserialization**: With serialization, a **Java Virtual Machine (JVM)** can write out the state of the object to some stream so that we can basically read all the members and write out their state to a stream, disk, and so on. The default mechanism is in a binary format so it's more compact than the textual format. Through this, machines can send data across the network. Deserialization is vice versa and is used for receiving data objects over the network.

- **Java generics**: This allows a type or method to operate on objects of various types while providing compile-time type safety, making Java a fully static typed language.

- **Java collection**: This framework is a set of classes and interfaces for handling various types of data collection with single Java objects.

- **Java concurrency**: This has been designed to support concurrent programming, and all execution takes place in the context of threads. It is mainly used for implementing computational processes as a set of threads within a single operating system process.

- **Plain Old Java Objects (POJO)**: These are actually ordinary JavaBeans. POJO is temporarily used for setting up as well as retrieving the value of data objects.

Understanding the Hadoop MapReduce fundamentals

To understand Hadoop MapReduce fundamentals properly, we will:

- Understand MapReduce objects
- Learn how to decide the number of Maps in MapReduce
- Learn how to decide the number of Reduces in MapReduce
- Understand MapReduce dataflow
- Take a closer look at Hadoop MapReduce terminologies

Understanding MapReduce objects

As we know, MapReduce operations in Hadoop are carried out mainly by three objects: Mapper, Reducer, and Driver.

- **Mapper**: This is designed for the Map phase of MapReduce, which starts MapReduce operations by carrying input files and splitting them into several pieces. For each piece, it will emit a key-value data pair as the output value.

- **Reducer**: This is designed for the Reduce phase of a MapReduce job; it accepts key-based grouped data from the Mapper output, reduces it by aggregation logic, and emits the (key, value) pair for the group of values.

- **Driver**: This is the main file that drives the MapReduce process. It starts the execution of MapReduce tasks after getting a request from the client application with parameters. The Driver file is responsible for building the configuration of a job and submitting it to the Hadoop cluster. The Driver code will contain the main() method that accepts arguments from the command line. The input and output directory of the Hadoop MapReduce job will be accepted by this program. Driver is the main file for defining job configuration details, such as the job name, job input format, job output format, and the Mapper, Combiner, Partitioner, and Reducer classes. MapReduce is initialized by calling this main() function of the Driver class.

Not every problem can be solved with a single Map and single Reduce program, but fewer can't be solved with a single Map and single Reduce task. Sometimes, it is also necessary to design the MapReduce job with multiple Map and Reduce tasks. We can design this type of job when we need to perform data operations, such as data extraction, data cleaning, and data merging, together in a single job. Many problems can be solved by writing multiple Mapper and Reducer tasks for a single job. The MapReduce steps that will be called sequentially in the case of multiple Map and Reduce tasks are Map1 followed by Reduce1, Map2 followed by Reduce2, and so on.

When we need to write a MapReduce job with multiple Map and Reduce tasks, we have to write multiple MapReduce application drivers to run them sequentially.

At the time of the MapReduce job submission, we can provide a number of Map tasks, and a number of Reducers will be created based on the output from the Mapper input and Hadoop cluster capacity. Also, note that setting the number of Mappers and Reducers is not mandatory.

Deciding the number of Maps in MapReduce

The number of Maps is usually defined by the size of the input data and size of the data split block that is calculated by the size of the HDFS file / data split. Therefore, if we have an HDFS datafile of 5 TB and a block size of 128 MB, there will be 40,960 maps present in the file. But sometimes, the number of Mappers created will be more than this count because of speculative execution. This is true when the input is a file, though it entirely depends on the `InputFormat` class.

In Hadoop MapReduce processing, there will be a delay in the result of the job when the assigned Mapper or Reducer is taking a long time to finish. If you want to avoid this, speculative execution in Hadoop can run multiple copies of the same Map or Reduce task on different nodes, and the result from the first completed nodes can be used. From the Hadoop API with the `setNumMapTasks(int)` method, we can get an idea of the number of Mappers.

Deciding the number of Reducers in MapReduce

A numbers of Reducers are created based on the Mapper's input. However, if you hardcode the number of Reducers in MapReduce, it won't matter how many nodes are present in a cluster. It will be executed as specified in the configuration.

Additionally, we can set the number of Reducers at runtime along with the MapReduce command at the command prompt `-D mapred.reduce.tasks`, with the number you want. Programmatically, it can be set via `conf.setNumReduceTasks(int)`.

Understanding MapReduce dataflow

Now that we have seen the components that make a basic MapReduce job possible, we will distinguish how everything works together at a higher level. From the following diagram, we will understand MapReduce dataflow with multiple nodes in a Hadoop cluster:

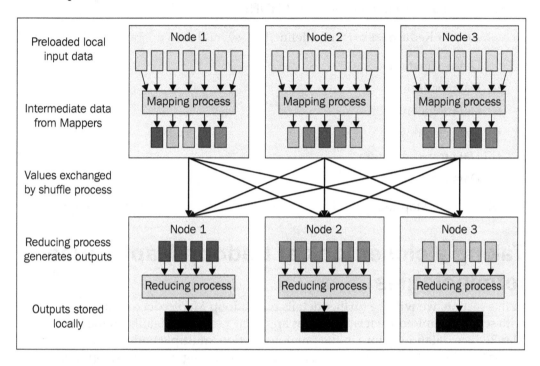

MapReduce dataflow

The two APIs available for Hadoop MapReduce are: New (Hadoop 1.x and 2.x) and Old Hadoop (0.20). YARN is the next generation of Hadoop MapReduce and the new Apache Hadoop subproject that has been released for Hadoop resource management.

Hadoop data processing includes several tasks that help achieve the final output from an input dataset. These tasks are as follows:

1. Preloading data in HDFS.

2. Running MapReduce by calling Driver.

3. Reading of input data by the Mappers, which results in the splitting of the data execution of the Mapper custom logic and the generation of intermediate key-value pairs

4. Executing Combiner and the shuffle phase to optimize the overall Hadoop MapReduce process.

5. Sorting and providing of intermediate key-value pairs to the Reduce phase. The Reduce phase is then executed. Reducers take these partitioned key-value pairs and aggregate them based on Reducer logic.

6. The final output data is stored at HDFS.

Here, Map and Reduce tasks can be defined for several data operations as follows:

- Data extraction
- Data loading
- Data segmentation
- Data cleaning
- Data transformation
- Data integration

We will explore MapReduce tasks in more detail in the next part of this chapter.

Taking a closer look at Hadoop MapReduce terminologies

In this section, we will see further details on Hadoop MapReduce dataflow with several MapReduce terminologies and their Java class details. In the MapReduce dataflow figure in the previous section, multiple nodes are connected across the network for performing distributed processing with a Hadoop setup. The ensuing attributes of the Map and Reduce phases play an important role for getting the final output.

The attributes of the Map phase are as follows:

- The `InputFiles` term refers to input, raw datasets that have been created/extracted to be analyzed for business analytics, which have been stored in HDFS. These input files are very large, and they are available in several types.

- The `InputFormat` is a Java class to process the input files by obtaining the text of each line of offset and the contents. It defines how to split and read input data files. We can set the several input types, such as `TextInputFormat`, `KeyValueInputFormat`, and `SequenceFileInputFormat`, of the input format that are relevant to the Map and Reduce phase.

- The InputSplits class is used for setting the size of the data split.

- The RecordReader is a Java class that comes with several methods to retrieve key and values by iterating them among the data splits. Also, it includes other methods to get the status on the current progress.

- The Mapper instance is created for the Map phase. The Mapper class takes input (key, value) pairs (generated by RecordReader) and produces an intermediate (key, value) pair by performing user-defined code in a Map() method. The Map() method mainly takes two input parameters: key and value; the remaining ones are OutputCollector and Reporter. OutputCollector. They will provide intermediate the key-value pair to reduce the phase of the job. Reporter provides the status of the current job to JobTracker periodically. The JobTracker will aggregate them for later retrieval when the job ends.

The attributes of the Reduce phase are as follows:

- After completing the Map phase, the generated intermediate (key, value) pairs are partitioned based on a key attribute similarity consideration in the hash function. So, each Map task may emit (key, value) pairs to partition; all values for the same key are always reduced together without it caring about which Mapper is its origin. This partitioning and shuffling will be done automatically by the MapReduce job after the completion of the Map phase. There is no need to call them separately. Also, we can explicitly override their logic code as per the requirements of the MapReduce job.

- After completing partitioning and shuffling and before initializing the Reduce task, the intermediate (key, value) pairs are sorted based on a key attribute value by the Hadoop MapReduce job.

- The Reduce instance is created for the Reduce phase. It is a section of user-provided code that performs the Reduce task. A Reduce() method of the Reducer class mainly takes two parameters along with OutputCollector and Reporter, which is the same as the Map() function. They are the OutputCollector and Reporter objects. OutputCollector in both Map and Reduce has the same functionality, but in the Reduce phase, OutputCollector provides output to either the next Map phase (in case of multiple map and Reduce job combinations) or reports it as the final output of the jobs based on the requirement. Apart from that, Reporter periodically reports to JobTracker about the current status of the running task.

- Finally, in `OutputFormat` the generated output (key, value) pairs are provided to the `OutputCollector` parameter and then written to `OutputFiles`, which is governed by `OutputFormat`. It controls the setting of the `OutputFiles` format as defined in the MapReduce Driver. The format will be chosen from either `TextOutputFormat`, `SequenceFileOutputFileFormat`, or `NullOutputFormat`.

- The factory `RecordWriter` used by `OutputFormat` to write the output data in the appropriate format.

- The output files are the output data written to HDFS by `RecordWriter` after the completion of the MapReduce job.

To run this MapReduce job efficiently, we need to have some knowledge of Hadoop shell commands to perform administrative tasks. Refer to the following table:

Shell commands	Usage and code sample
cat	To copy source paths to `stdout`:
	`Hadoop fs -cat URI [URI …]`
chmod	To change the permissions of files:
	`Hadoop fs -chmod [-R] <MODE[,MODE]...	OCTALMODE> URI [URI …]`
copyFromLocal	To copy a file from local storage to HDFS:
	`Hadoop fs -copyFromLocal<localsrc> URI`
copyToLocal	To copy a file from HDFS to local storage:
	`Hadoop fs -copyToLocal [-ignorecrc] [-crc] URI <localdst>`
cp	To copy a file from the source to the destination in HDFS:
	`Hadoop fs -cp URI [URI …] <dest>`
du	To display the aggregate length of a file:
	`Hadoop fs -du URI [URI …]`
dus	To display the summary of file length:
	`Hadoop fs -dus<args>`
get	To copy files to a local filesystem:
	`Hadoop fs -get [-ignorecrc] [-crc] <src><localdst>`
ls	To list all files in the current directory in HDFS:
	`Hadoop fs -ls<args>`
mkdir	To create a directory in HDFS:
	`Hadoop fs -mkdir<paths>`

Shell commands	Usage and code sample
`lv`	To move files from the source to the destination:
	`Hadoop fs -mv URI [URI ...] <dest>`
`rmr`	To remove files from the current directory:
	`Hadoop fs -rmr URI [URI ...]`
`setrep`	To change the replication factor of a file:
	`Hadoop fs -setrep [-R] <path>`
`tail`	To display the last kilobyte of a file to `stdout`:
	`Hadoop fs -tail [-f] URI`

Writing a Hadoop MapReduce example

Now we will move forward with MapReduce by learning a very common and easy example of word count. The goal of this example is to calculate how many times each word occurs in the provided documents. These documents can be considered as input to MapReduce's file.

In this example, we already have a set of text files—we want to identify the frequency of all the unique words existing in the files. We will get this by designing the Hadoop MapReduce phase.

In this section, we will see more on Hadoop MapReduce programming using Hadoop MapReduce's old API. Here we assume that the reader has already set up the Hadoop environment as described in *Chapter 1, Getting Ready to Use R and Hadoop*. Also, keep in mind that we are not going to use R to count words; only Hadoop will be used here.

Basically, Hadoop MapReduce has three main objects: Mapper, Reducer, and Driver. They can be developed with three Java classes; they are the `Map` class, `Reduce` class, and `Driver` class, where the `Map` class denotes the Map phase, the `Reducer` class denotes the Reduce phase, and the `Driver` class denotes the class with the `main()` method to initialize the Hadoop MapReduce program.

In the previous section of Hadoop MapReduce fundamentals, we already discussed what Mapper, Reducer, and Driver are. Now, we will learn how to define them and program for them in Java. In upcoming chapters, we will be learning to do more with a combination of R and Hadoop.

There are many languages and frameworks that are used for building MapReduce, but each of them has different strengths. There are multiple factors that by modification can provide high latency over MapReduce. Refer to the article *10 MapReduce Tips* by Cloudera at `http://blog.cloudera.com/blog/2009/05/10-mapreduce-tips/`.

To make MapReduce development easier, use **Eclipse** configured with **Maven**, which supports the old MapReduce API.

Understanding the steps to run a MapReduce job

Let's see the steps to run a MapReduce job with Hadoop:

1. In the initial steps of preparing Java classes, we need you to develop a Hadoop MapReduce program as per the definition of our business problem. In this example, we have considered a word count problem. So, we have developed three Java classes for the MapReduce program; they are Map. java, Reduce. java, and WordCount. java, used for calculating the frequency of the word in the provided text files.

    °   Map.java: This is the Map class for the word count Mapper.

```
// Defining package of the class
package com.PACKT.chapter1;

// Importing java libraries
import java.io.*;
importjava.util.*;
import org.apache.hadoop.io.*;
import org.apache.hadoop.mapred.*;

// Defining the Map class
public class Map extends MapReduceBase implements
        Mapper<LongWritable,
                Text,
                Text,
                IntWritable>{

//Defining the map method - for processing the data with //
problem specific logic
public void map(LongWritable key,
                Text value,
                OutputCollector<Text,
```

```
                 IntWritable> output,
                 Reporter reporter)
                 throws IOException {

// For breaking the string to tokens and convert them to
lowercase
StringTokenizer st = new StringTokenizer(value.toString().
toLowerCase());

// For every string tokens
while(st.hasMoreTokens()) {

// Emitting the (key,value) pair with value 1.
output.collect(new Text(st.nextToken()),
            new IntWritable(1));
    }

  }

}
```

  ° Reduce.java: **This is the Reduce class for the word count Reducer.**

```
// Defining package of the class
package com.PACKT.chapter1;

// Importing java libraries
import java.io.*;
importjava.util.*;
import org.apache.hadoop.io.*;
importorg.apache.hadoop.mapred.*;

// Defining the Reduce class
public class Reduce extends MapReduceBase implements
        Reducer<Text,
                IntWritable,
                Text,
                IntWritable> {

// Defining the reduce method for aggregating the //
generated output of Map phase
public void reduce(Text key,
                Iterator<IntWritable> values,
                OutputCollector<Text,IntWritable>
                output,
                Reporter reporter) throws IOException {
```

```
// Setting initial counter value as 0
int count = 0;

// For every element with similar key attribute, increment
its counter value by adding 1.
while(values.hasNext()) {
count += values.next().get();
        }

// Emitting the (key,value) pair
output.collect(key, new IntWritable(count));
    }
}
```

°   WordCount.java: **This is the task of Driver in the Hadoop MapReduce Driver main file.**

```
//Defining package of the class
package com.PACKT.chapter1;

// Importing java libraries
import java.io.*;
importorg.apache.hadoop.fs.*;
import org.apache.hadoop.io.*;
importorg.apache.hadoop.mapred.*;
importorg.apache.hadoop.util.*;
importorg.apache.hadoop.conf.*;

//Defining wordcount class for job configuration
  // information
public class WordCount extends Configured implements Tool{

publicint run(String[] args) throws IOException{
JobConfconf = new JobConf(WordCount.class);
conf.setJobName("wordcount");

//For defining the output key format
conf.setOutputKeyClass(Text.class);

//For defining the output value format
conf.setOutputValueClass(IntWritable.class);

// For defining the Mapper class implementation
conf.setMapperClass(Map.class);
```

```
// For defining the Reducer class implementation
conf.setReducerClass(Reduce.class);

// For defining the type of input format
conf.setInputFormat(TextInputFormat.class);

// For defining the type of output format
conf.setOutputFormat(TextOutputFormat.class);

// For defining the command line argument sequence for //
input dataset path
FileInputFormat.setInputPaths(conf, new Path(args[0]));

// For defining the command line argument sequence for //
output dataset path
FileOutputFormat.setOutputPath(conf, new Path(args[1]));


// For submitting the configuration object
JobClient.runJob(conf);

return 0;
    }

// Defining the main() method to start the execution of //
the MapReduce program
public static void main(String[] args) throws Exception {
   intexitCode = ToolRunner.run(new WordCount(), args);
   System.exit(exitCode); } }
```

2. Compile the Java classes.

    ```
    // create a folder for storing the compiled classes
    hduser@ubuntu:~/Desktop/PacktPub$ mkdir classes

    // compile the java class files with classpath
    hduser@ubuntu:~/Desktop/PacktPub$ javac -classpath /usr/local/
    hadoop/hadoop-core-1.1.0.jar:/usr/local/hadoop/lib/commons-cli-
    1.2.jar -d classes *.java
    ```

3. Create a `.jar` file from the compiled classes.

   ```
   hduser@ubuntu:~/Desktop/PacktPub$ cd classes/

   // create jar of developed java classes
   hduser@ubuntu:~/Desktop/PacktPub/classes$ jar -cvf wordcount.jar
   com
   ```

4. Start the Hadoop daemons.

   ```
   // Go to Hadoop home Directory
   hduser@ubuntu:~$ cd $HADOOP_HOME

   // Start Hadoop Cluster
   hduser@ubuntu:/usr/local/hadoop$ bin/start-all.sh
   ```

5. Check all the running daemons.

   ```
   // Ensure all daemons are running properly
   hduser@ubuntu:/usr/local/hadoop$ jps
   ```

6. Create the HDFS directory /wordcount/input/.

   ```
   // Create Hadoop directory for storing the input dataset
   hduser@ubuntu:/usr/local/hadoop$ bin/Hadoop fs -mkdir /wordcount/
   input
   ```

7. Extract the input dataset to be used in the word count example. As we need to have text files to be processed by the word count example, we will use the text files provided with the Hadoop distribution (CHANGES. txt, LICENSE.txt, NOTICE.txt, and README.txt) by copying them to the Hadoop directory. We can have other text datasets from the Internet input in this MapReduce algorithm instead of using readymade text files. We can also extract data from the Internet to process them, but here we are using readymade input files.

8. Copy all the text files to HDFS.

```
// To copying the text files from machine's local
  // directory in to Hadoop directory

hduser@ubuntu:/usr/local/hadoop$ bin/hadoopfs -copyFromLocal
$HADOOP_HOME/*.txt /wordcount/input/
```

9. Run the Hadoop MapReduce job with the following command:

```
// Command for running the Hadoop job by specifying jar, main
class, input directory and output directory.

hduser@ubuntu:/usr/local/hadoop$ bin/hadoop jar wordcount.jar com.
PACKT.chapter1.WordCount /wordcount/input/ /wordcount/output/
```

10. This is how the final output will look.

```
// To read the generated output from HDFS directory

hduser@ubuntu:/usr/local/hadoop$ bin/hadoopfs -cat /wordcount/
output/part-00000
```

> During the MapReduce phase, you need to monitor the job as well as the nodes. Use the following to monitor MapReduce jobs in web browsers:
>
> - localhost:50070: NameNode Web interface (for HDFS)
> - localhost:50030: JobTracker Web interface (for MapReduce layer)
> - localhost:50060: TaskTracker Web interface (for MapReduce layer)

Learning to monitor and debug a Hadoop MapReduce job

In this section, we will learn how to monitor as well as debug a Hadoop MapReduce job without any commands.

This is one of the easiest ways to use the Hadoop MapReduce administration UI. We can access this via a browser by entering the URL `http://localhost:50030` (web UI for the JobTracker daemon). This will show the logged information of the Hadoop MapReduce jobs, which looks like following screenshot:

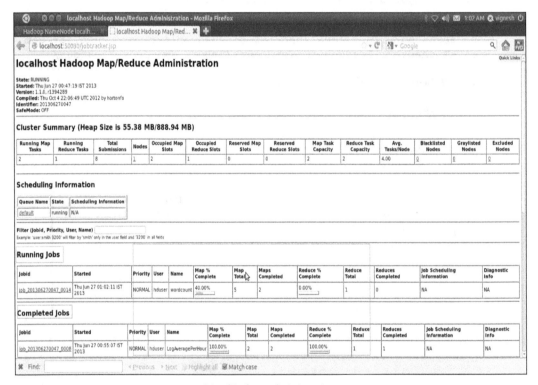

Map/Reduce administration

Here we can check the information and status of running jobs, the status of the Map and Reduce tasks of a job, and the past completed jobs as well as failed jobs with failed Map and Reduce tasks. Additionally, we can debug a MapReduce job by clicking on the hyperlink of the failed Map or Reduce task of the failed job. This will produce an error message printed on standard output while the job is running.

Exploring HDFS data

In this section, we will see how to explore HDFS directories without running any **Bash** command. The web UI of the NameNode daemon provides such a facility. We just need to locate it at http://localhost:50070.

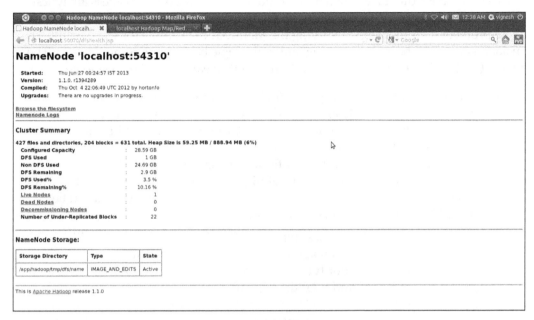

NameNode administration

This UI enables us to get a cluster summary (memory status), NameNode logs, as well as information on live and dead nodes in the cluster. Also, this allows us to explore the Hadoop directory that we have created for storing input and output data for Hadoop MapReduce jobs.

Understanding several possible MapReduce definitions to solve business problems

Until now we have learned what MapReduce is and how to code it. Now, we will see some common MapReduce problem definitions that are used for business analytics. Any reader who knows MapReduce with Hadoop will easily be able to code and solve these problem definitions by modifying the MapReduce example for word count. The major changes will be in data parsing and in the logic behind operating the data. The major effort will be required in data collection, data cleaning, and data storage.

- **Server web log processing**: Through this MapReduce definition, we can perform web log analysis. Logs of the web server provide information about web requests, such as requested page's URL, date, time, and protocol. From this, we can identify the peak load hours of our website from the web server log and scale our web server configuration based on the traffic on the site. So, the identification of no traffic at night will help us save money by scaling down the server. Also, there are a number of business cases that can be solved by this web log server analysis.

- **Web analytics with website statistics**: Website statistics can provide more detailed information about the visitor's metadata, such as the source, campaign, visitor type, visitor location, search keyword, requested page URL, browser, and total time spent on pages. Google analytics is one of the popular, free service providers for websites. By analyzing all this information, we can understand visitors' behavior on a website. By descriptive analytics, we can identify the importance of web pages or other web attributes based on visitors' addiction towards them. For an e-commerce website, we can identify popular products based on the total number of visits, page views, and time spent by a visitor on a page. Also, predictive analytics can be implemented on web data to predict the business.

- **Search engine**: Suppose we have a large set of documents and want to search the document for a specific keyword, inverted indices with Hadoop MapReduce will help us find keywords so we can build a search engine for Big Data.

- **Stock market analysis**: Let's say that we have collected stock market data (Big Data) for a long period of time and now want to identify the pattern and predict it for the next time period. This requires training of all historical datasets. Then we can compute the frequency of the stock market changes for the said time period using several machine-learning libraries with Hadoop MapReduce.

Also, there are too many possible MapReduce applications that can be applied to improve business cost.

Learning the different ways to write Hadoop MapReduce in R

We know that Hadoop Big Data processing with MapReduce is a big deal for statisticians, web analysts, and product managers who used to use the R tool for analyses because supplementary programming knowledge of MapReduce is required to migrate the analyses into MapReduce with Hadoop. Also, we know R is a tool that is consistently increasing in popularity; there are many packages/libraries that are being developed for integrating with R. So to develop a MapReduce algorithm or program that runs with the log of R and computation power of Hadoop, we require the middleware for R and Hadoop. RHadoop, RHIPE, and Hadoop streaming are the middleware that help develop and execute Hadoop MapReduce within R. In this last section, we will talk about RHadoop, RHIPE, and introducing Hadoop streaming, and from the later chapters we will purely develop MapReduce with these packages.

Learning RHadoop

RHadoop is a great open source software framework of R for performing data analytics with the Hadoop platform via R functions. RHadoop has been developed by **Revolution Analytics**, which is the leading commercial provider of software and services based on the open source R project for statistical computing. The RHadoop project has three different R packages: rhdfs, rmr, and rhbase. All these packages are implemented and tested on the Cloudera Hadoop distributions CDH3, CDH4, and R 2.15.0. Also, these are tested with the R version 4.3, 5.0, and 6.0 distributions of Revolution Analytics.

These three different R packages have been designed on Hadoop's two main features HDFS and MapReduce:

- rhdfs: This is an R package for providing all Hadoop HDFS access to R. All distributed files can be managed with R functions.

- rmr: This is an R package for providing Hadoop MapReduce interfaces to R. With the help of this package, the Mapper and Reducer can easily be developed.

- rhbase: This is an R package for handling data at HBase distributed database through R.

Learning RHIPE

R and Hadoop Integrated Programming Environment (**RHIPE**) is a free and open source project. RHIPE is widely used for performing Big Data analysis with **D&R** analysis. D&R analysis is used to divide huge data, process it in parallel on a distributed network to produce intermediate output, and finally recombine all this intermediate output into a set. RHIPE is designed to carry out D&R analysis on complex Big Data in R on the Hadoop platform. RHIPE was developed by *Saptarshi Joy Guha* (Data Analyst at Mozilla Corporation) and her team as part of her PhD thesis in the Purdue Statistics Department.

Learning Hadoop streaming

Hadoop streaming is a utility that comes with the Hadoop distribution. This utility allows you to create and run MapReduce jobs with any executable or script as the Mapper and/or Reducer. This is supported by R, Python, Ruby, Bash, Perl, and so on. We will use the R language with a bash script.

Also, there is one R package named `HadoopStreaming` that has been developed for performing data analysis on Hadoop clusters with the help of R scripts, which is an interface to Hadoop streaming with R. Additionally, it also allows the running of MapReduce tasks without Hadoop. This package was developed by *David Rosenberg*, Chief Scientist at SenseNetworks. He has expertise in machine learning and statistical modeling.

Summary

In this chapter, we have seen what Hadoop MapReduce is, and how to develop it as well as run it. In the next chapter, we will learn how to install RHIPE and RHadoop, and develop MapReduce and its available functional libraries with examples.

Integrating R and Hadoop

3

From the first two chapters we got basic information on how to install the R and Hadoop tools. Also, we learned what the key features of Hadoop are and why they are integrated with R for Big Data solutions to business data problems. So with the integration of R and Hadoop we can forward data analytics to Big Data analytics. Both of these middleware are still getting improved for being used along with each other.

In *Chapter 2, Writing Hadoop MapReduce Programs*, we learned how to write a MapReduce program in Hadoop. In this chapter, we will learn to develop the MapReduce programs in R that run over the Hadoop cluster. This chapter will provide development tutorials on R and Hadoop with RHIPE and RHadoop. After installing R and Hadoop, we will see how R and Hadoop can be integrated using easy steps.

Before we start moving on to the installation, let's see what are the advantages of R and Hadoop integration within an organization. Since statisticians and data analysts frequently use the R tool for data exploration as well as data analytics, Hadoop integration is a big boon for processing large-size data. Similarly, data engineers who use Hadoop tools, such as system, to organize the data warehouse can perform such logical analytical operations to get informative insights that are actionable by integrating with R tool.

Therefore, the integration of such data-driven tools and technologies can build a powerful scalable system that has features of both of them.

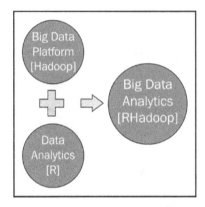

Three ways to link R and Hadoop are as follows:

- RHIPE
- RHadoop
- Hadoop streaming

In this chapter, we will be learning integration and analytics with RHIPE and RHadoop. Hadoop streaming will be covered in *Chapter 4, Using Hadoop Streaming with R.*

Introducing RHIPE

RHIPE stands for **R and Hadoop Integrated Programming Environment**. As mentioned on http://www.datadr.org/, it means "in a moment" in Greek and is a merger of R and Hadoop. It was first developed by *Saptarshi Guha* for his PhD thesis in the Department of Statistics at Purdue University in 2012. Currently this is carried out by the Department of Statistics team at Purdue University and other active Google discussion groups.

The RHIPE package uses the **Divide and Recombine** technique to perform data analytics over Big Data. In this technique, data is divided into subsets, computation is performed over those subsets by specific R analytics operations, and the output is combined. RHIPE has mainly been designed to accomplish two goals that are as follows:

- Allowing you to perform in-depth analysis of large as well as small data.
- Allowing users to perform the analytics operations within R using a lower-level language. RHIPE is designed with several functions that help perform **Hadoop Distribute File System** (**HDFS**) as well as MapReduce operations using a simple R console.

RHIPE is a lower-level interface as compared to HDFS and MapReduce operation. Use the latest supported version of RHIPE which is 0.73.1 as `Rhipe_0.73.1-2.tar.gz`.

Installing RHIPE

As RHIPE is a connector of R and Hadoop, we need Hadoop and R installed on our machine or in our clusters in the following sequence:

1. Installing Hadoop.
2. Installing R.
3. Installing protocol buffers.
4. Setting up environment variables.
5. Installing rJava.
6. Installing RHIPE.

Let us begin with the installation.

Installing Hadoop

As we are here to integrate R and Hadoop with the RHIPE package library, we need to install Hadoop on our machine. It will be arbitrary that it either be a single node or multinode installation depending on the size of the data to be analyzed.

As we have already learned how to install Hadoop in Ubuntu, we are not going to repeat the process here. If you haven't installed it yet, please refer to *Chapter 1, Getting Ready to Use R and Hadoop*, for guidance.

Installing R

If we use a multinode Hadoop architecture, there are a number of TaskTracker nodes for executing the MapReduce job. So, we need to install R over all of these TaskTracker nodes. These TaskTracker nodes will start process over the data subsets with developed map and reduce logic with the consideration of key values.

Installing protocol buffers

Protocol buffers just serialize the data to make it platform independent, neutral, and robust (primarily used for structured data). Google uses the same protocol for data interchange. RHIPE depends on protocol buffers 2.4.1 for data serialization over the network.

This can be installed using the following command:

```
## For downloading the protocol buffer 2.4.1
wget http://protobuf.googlecode.com/files/protobuf-2.4.1.tar.gz


## To extracting the protocol buffer
tar -xzf protobuf-2.4.1.tar.gz


## To get in to the extracted protocol buffer directory
cd protobuf-2.4.1


## For making install the protocol buffer
./configure # --prefix=...
make
make install
```

Environment variables

In order for RHIPE to compile and work correctly, it is better to ensure that the following environment variables are set appropriately:

For configuring the Hadoop libraries, we need to set two variables, `PKG_CONFIG_PATH` and `LD_LIBRARY_PATH`, to the `~./bashrc` file of `hduser` (Hadoop user) so that it can automatically be set when the user logs in to the system.

Here, `PKG_CONFIG_PATH` is an environment variable that holds the path of the `pkg-config` script for retrieving information about installed libraries in the system, and `LD_LIBRARY_PATH` is an environment variable that holds the path of native shared libraries.

```
export PKG_CONFIG_PATH = /usr/local/lib
export LD_LIBRARY_PATH = /usr/local/lib
```

You can also set all these variables from your R console, as follows:

```
Sys.setenv(HADOOP_HOME="/usr/local/hadoop/")
Sys.setenv(HADOOP_BIN="/usr/local/hadoop/bin")
Sys.setenv(HADOOP_CONF_DIR="/usr/local/hadoop/conf")
```

Where `HADOOP_HOME` is used for specifying the location of the Hadoop directory, `HADOOP_BIN` is used for specifying the location of binary files of Hadoop, and `HADOOP_CONF_DIR` is used for specifying the configuration files of Hadoop.

Setting the variables is temporary and valid up to a particular R session. If we want to make this variable permanent, as initialized automatically when the R session initializes, we need to set these variables to the `/etc/R/Renviron` file as we set the environment variable in `.bashrc` of a specific user profile.

The rJava package installation

Since RHIPE is a Java package, it acts like a Java bridge between R and Hadoop. RHIPE serializes the input data to a Java type, which has to be serialized over the cluster. It needs a low-level interface to Java, which is provided by rJava. So, we will install rJava to enable the functioning of RHIPE.

```
## For installing the rJava Package will be used for calling java
libraries from R.
install.packages("rJava")
```

Installing RHIPE

Now, it's time to install the RHIPE package from its repository.

```
## Downloading RHIPE package from RHIPE repository
Wget http://ml.stat.purdue.edu/rhipebin/Rhipe_0.73.1-2.tar.gz

## Installing the RHIPE package in R via CMD command
R CMD INSTALL Rhipe_0.73.1.tar.gz
```

Now, we are ready with a RHIPE system for performing data analytics with R and Hadoop.

Understanding the architecture of RHIPE

Let's understand the working of the RHIPE library package developed to integrate R and Hadoop for effective Big Data analytics.

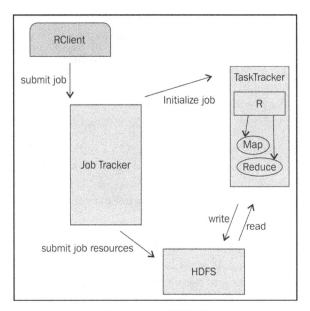

Components of RHIPE

There are a number of Hadoop components that will be used for data analytics operations with R and Hadoop.

The components of RHIPE are as follows:

- **RClient**: RClient is an R application that calls the **JobTracker** to execute the job with an indication of several MapReduce job resources such as Mapper, Reducer, input format, output format, input file, output file, and other several parameters that can handle the MapReduce jobs with RClient.

- **JobTracker**: A JobTracker is the master node of the Hadoop MapReduce operations for initializing and monitoring the MapReduce jobs over the Hadoop cluster.

- **TaskTracker**: TaskTracker is a slave node in the Hadoop cluster. It executes the MapReduce jobs as per the orders given by JobTracker, retrieve the input data chunks, and run R-specific `Mapper` and `Reducer` over it. Finally, the output will be written on the HDFS directory.

- **HDFS**: HDFS is a filesystem distributed over Hadoop clusters with several data nodes. It provides data services for various data operations.

Understanding RHIPE samples

In this section, we will create two RHIPE MapReduce examples. These two examples are defined with the basic utility of the Hadoop MapReduce job from a RHIPE package.

RHIPE sample program (Map only)

MapReduce problem definition: The goal of this MapReduce sample program is to test the RHIPE installation by using the `min` and `max` functions over numeric data with the Hadoop environment. Since this is a sample program, we have included only the Map phase, which will store its output in the HDFS directory.

To start the development with RHIPE, we need to initialize the RHIPE subsystem by loading the library and calling the `rhinit()` method.

```
## Loading the RHIPE library
library(Rhipe)
```

```
## initializing the RHIPE subsystem, which is used for everything. RHIPE
will not work if rhinit is not called.
rhinit()
```

Input: We insert a numerical value rather than using a file as an input.

Map phase: The Map phase of this MapReduce program will call 10 different iterations and in all of those iterations, random numbers from 1 to 10 will be generated as per their iteration number. After that, the max and min values for that generated numbers will be calculated.

```
## Defining the Map phase
```

```
Map(function(k,v){
```

```
## for generating the random deviates
  X   runif(v)
```

```
## for emitting the key-value pairs with key - k and
## value - min and max of generated random deviates.
  rhcollect(k,  c(Min=min(x),Max=max(x)))
}
```

Output: Finally the output of the Map phase will be considered here as an output of this MapReduce job and it will be stored to HDFS at `/app/hadoop/RHIPE/`.

Defining the MapReduce job by the `rhwatch()` method of the RHIPE package:

```
## Create and running a MapReduce job by following
job = rhwatch(map=map,input=10,reduce=0,
output="/app/Hadoop/RHIPE/test",jobname='test')
```

Reading the MapReduce output from HDFS:

```
## Read the results of job from HDFS
result <- rhread(job)
```

For displaying the result in a more readable form in the table format, use the following code:

```
## Displaying the result
outputdata  <- do.call('rbind', lapply(result, "[[", 2))
```

Output:

```
> ## Displaying the result
> outputdata  <- do.call('rbind', lapply(result, "[[", 2))
> outputdata
        n        Min        Max
 [1,]   1 0.21168294 0.2116829
 [2,]   2 0.31025842 0.5790579
 [3,]   3 0.00842532 0.8953705
 [4,]   4 0.22550440 0.8315111
 [5,]   5 0.22385646 0.9643431
 [6,]   6 0.06959446 0.9336256
 [7,]   7 0.09994765 0.7005731
 [8,]   8 0.01904263 0.7651515
 [9,]   9 0.07743241 0.9330207
[10,]  10 0.40015677 0.9349429
>
```

Word count

MapReduce problem definition: This RHIPE MapReduce program is defined for identifying the frequency of all of the words that are present in the provided input text files.

Also note that this is the same MapReduce problem as we saw in *Chapter 2, Writing Hadoop MapReduce Programs*.

```
## Loading the RHIPE Library
library(Rhipe)
```

Input: We will use the CHANGES.txt file, which comes with Hadoop distribution, and use it with this MapReduce algorithm. By using the following command, we will copy it to HDFS:

```
rhput("/usr/local/hadoop/CHANGES.txt","/RHIPE/input/")
```

Map phase: The Map phase contains the code for reading all the words from a file and assigning all of them to value 1.

```
## Defining the Map function
w_map<-expression({
  words_vector<-unlist(strsplit(unlist(map.values)," "))
  lapply(words_vector,function(i) rhcollect(i,1))
})
```

Reduce phase: With this reducer task, we can calculate the total frequency of the words in the input text files.

```
## For reference, RHIPE provides a canned version
Reduce = rhoptions()$templates$scalarsummer


## Defining the Reduce function
w_reduce<-expression(
  pre={total=0},
  reduce={total<-sum(total,unlist(reduce.values))},
  post={rhcollect(reduce.key,total)}
)
```

Defining the MapReduce job object: After defining the word count mapper and reducer, we need to design the `driver` method that can execute this MapReduce job by calling `Mapper` and `Reducer` sequentially.

```
## defining and executing a MapReduce job object
Job1 <-
  rhwatch(map=w_map,reduce=w_reduce,
  ,input="/RHIPE/input/",output="/RHIPE/output/",
  jobname="word_count")
```

Reading the MapReduce output:

```
## for reading the job output data from HDFS
Output_data <- rhread(Job1)
results <- data.frame(words=unlist(lapply(Output_data,"[[",1)), count
=unlist(lapply(Output_data,"[[",2)))
```

The output of MapReduce job will be stored to `output_data`, we will convert this output into R supported dataframe format. The dataframe output will be stored to the `results` variable. For displaying the MapReduce output in the data frame the format will be as follows:

Output for `head (results)`:

```
> head(results)
  words count
1       30780
2    \t     3
3     #     1
4     %     4
5     &    26
6     *     4
```

Output for `tail (results)`:

```
> tail(results)
                                                        words count
12783            org.apache.hadoop.security.AccessControlIOException      1
12784            org.apache.hadoop.security.JniBasedUnixGroupsMapping     1
12785            com.sun.jersey.api.ParamException$QueryParamException    1
12786            http://svn.apache.org/viewvc?view=rev&revision=588771.   1
12787            org.apache.hadoop.fs.permission.AccessControlException   2
12788 org.apache.hadoop.record.compiler.generated.SimpleCharStream.      1
```

Understanding the RHIPE function reference

RHIPE is specially designed for providing a lower-level interface over Hadoop. So R users with a RHIPE package can easily fire the Hadoop data operations over large datasets that are stored on HDFS, just like the `print ()` function called in R.

Now we will see all the possible functional uses of all methods that are available in RHIPE library. All these methods are with three categories: Initialization, HDFS, and MapReduce operations.

Initialization

We use the following command for initialization:

- `rhinit`: This is used to initialize the Rhipe subsystem.

  `rhinit(TRUE,TRUE)`

HDFS

We use the following command for HDFS operations:

- `rhls`: This is used to retrieve all directories from HDFS.

  Its syntax is `rhls(path)`

  `rhls("/")`

Output:

```
> rhls("/")
  permission  owner      group size          modtime             file
1 drwxr-xr-x   root supergroup     0 2013-10-15 01:09            /RHIPE
2 drwxr-xr-x hduser supergroup     0 2013-10-15 00:49             /app
3 drwxr-xr-x hduser supergroup     0 2013-06-25 14:44             /foo
4 drwxr-xr-x   root supergroup     0 2013-07-23 01:36            /hdfs
5 drwxr-xr-x hduser supergroup     0 2013-07-28 02:34             /hds
6 drwxr-xr-x hduser supergroup     0 2013-06-27 00:55            /logs
7 drwxr-xr-x   root supergroup     0 2013-07-25 02:10        /output_02
8 drwxr-xr-x hduser supergroup     0 2013-06-25 14:45              /pc
9 drwxr-xr-x hduser supergroup     0 2013-08-18 14:09 /rhadoop_examples
10 drwxrwxr-x   root supergroup    0 2013-09-02 00:39             /tmp
11 drwxr-xr-x hduser supergroup    0 2013-08-18 14:08            /user
12 drwxr-xr-x hduser supergroup    0 2013-07-25 00:59             /usr
13 drwxr-xr-x hduser supergroup    0 2013-07-25 02:17       /wordcount
>
```

- `hdfs.getwd`: This is used for acquiring the current working HDFS directory. Its syntax is `hdfs.getwd()`

- `hdfs.setwd`: This is used for setting up the current working HDFS directory. Its syntax is `hdfs.setwd("/RHIPE")`

- `rhput`: This is used to copy a file from a local directory to HDFS. Its syntax is `rhput(src,dest)` and `rhput("/usr/local/hadoop/NOTICE.txt","/RHIPE/")`.

- `rhcp`: This is used to copy a file from one HDFS location to another HDFS location. Its syntax is `rhcp('/RHIPE/1/change.txt','/RHIPE/2/change.txt')`.

- `rhdel`: This is used to delete a directory/file from HDFS. Its syntax is `rhdel("/RHIPE/1")`.

- `rhget`: This is used to copy the HDFS file to a local directory. Its syntax is `rhget("/RHIPE/1/part-r-00000", "/usr/local/")`.

- `rwrite`: This is used to write the R data to HDFS. its syntax is `rhwrite(list(1,2,3),"/tmp/x")`.

MapReduce

We use the following commands for MapReduce operations:

- `rhwatch`: This is used to prepare, submit, and monitor MapReduce jobs.

```
# Syntax:
rhwatch(map, reduce, combiner, input, output,
mapred,partitioner,mapred, jobname)


## to prepare and submit MapReduce job:


z=rhwatch(map=map,reduce=0,input=5000,output="/tmp/
sort",mapred=mapred,read=FALSE)


results <- rhread(z)
```

- `rhex`: This is used to execute the MapReduce job from over Hadoop cluster.

```
## Submit the job
rhex(job)
```

- `rhjoin`: This is used to check whether the MapReduce job is completed or not. Its syntax is `rhjoin(job)`.

- `rhkill`: This is used to kill the running MapReduce job. Its syntax is `rhkill(job)`.

- `rhoptions`: This is used for getting or setting the RHIPE configuration options. Its syntax is `rhoptions()`.

- `rhstatus`: This is used to get the status of the RHIPE MapReduce job. Its syntax is `rhstatus(job)`.

```
rhstatus(job, mon.sec = 5, autokill = TRUE,
   showErrors = TRUE, verbose = FALSE, handler = NULL)
```

Introducing RHadoop

RHadoop is a collection of three R packages for providing large data operations with an R environment. It was developed by Revolution Analytics, which is the leading commercial provider of software based on R. RHadoop is available with three main R packages: rhdfs, rmr, and rhbase. Each of them offers different Hadoop features.

- rhdfs is an R interface for providing the HDFS usability from the R console. As Hadoop MapReduce programs write their output on HDFS, it is very easy to access them by calling the rhdfs methods. The R programmer can easily perform read and write operations on distributed data files. Basically, rhdfs package calls the HDFS API in backend to operate data sources stored on HDFS.

- rmr is an R interface for providing Hadoop MapReduce facility inside the R environment. So, the R programmer needs to just divide their application logic into the map and reduce phases and submit it with the rmr methods. After that, rmr calls the Hadoop streaming MapReduce API with several job parameters as input directory, output directory, mapper, reducer, and so on, to perform the R MapReduce job over Hadoop cluster.

- rhbase is an R interface for operating the Hadoop HBase data source stored at the distributed network via a Thrift server. The rhbase package is designed with several methods for initialization and read/write and table manipulation operations.

Here it's not necessary to install all of the three RHadoop packages to run the Hadoop MapReduce operations with R and Hadoop. If we have stored our input data source at the HBase data source, we need to install rhbase; else we require rhdfs and rmr packages. As Hadoop is most popular for its two main features, Hadoop MapReduce and HDFS, both of these features will be used within the R console with the help of RHadoop rhdfs and rmr packages. These packages are enough to run Hadoop MapReduce from R. Basically, rhdfs provides HDFS data operations while rmr provides MapReduce execution operations.

RHadoop also includes another package called quick check, which is designed for debugging the developed MapReduce job defined by the rmr package.

In the next section, we will see their architectural relationships as well as their installation steps.

Understanding the architecture of RHadoop

Since Hadoop is highly popular because of HDFS and MapReduce, Revolution Analytics has developed separate R packages, namely, `rhdfs`, `rmr`, and `rhbase`. The architecture of RHadoop is shown in the following diagram:

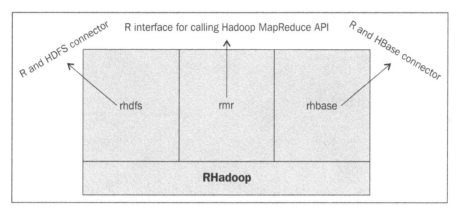

RHadoop Ecosystem

Installing RHadoop

In this section, we will learn some installation tricks for the three RHadoop packages including their prerequisites.

- **R and Hadoop installation**: As we are going to use an R and Hadoop integrated environment, we need Hadoop as well as R installed on our machine. If you haven't installed yet, see *Chapter 1, Getting Ready to Use R and Hadoop*. As we know, if we have too much data, we need to scale our cluster by increasing the number of nodes. Based on this, to get RHadoop installed on our system we need Hadoop with either a single node or multimode installation as per the size of our data.

  RHadoop is already tested with several Hadoop distributions provided by Cloudera, Hortonworks, and MapR.

- **Installing the R packages**: We need several R packages to be installed that help it to connect R with Hadoop. The list of the packages is as follows:
  - rJava
  - RJSONIO
  - itertools
  - digest
  - Rcpp
  - httr
  - functional
  - devtools
  - plyr
  - reshape2

  We can install them by calling the execution of the following R command in the R console:

  ```
  install.packages( c('rJava','RJSONIO', 'itertools', 'digest','Rcpp
  ','httr','functional','devtools', 'plyr','reshape2'))
  ```

- **Setting environment variables**: We can set this via the R console using the following code:

  ```
  ## Setting HADOOP_CMD
  ```
  ```
  Sys.setenv(HADOOP_CMD="/usr/local/hadoop/bin/hadoop")
  ```

  ```
  ## Setting up HADOOP_STREAMING
  ```
  ```
  Sys.setenv(HADOOP_STREAMING="/usr/local/hadoop/contrib/streaming/
  hadoop-streaming-1.0.3.jar")
  ```

  or, we can also set the R console via the command line as follows:

  ```
  export HADOOP_CMD=/usr/local/Hadoop
  ```
  ```
  export HADOOP_STREAMING=/usr/lib/hadoop-0.20-mapreduce/contrib/
  streaming/hadoop-streaming-2.0.0-mr1-cdh4.1.1.jar
  ```

- Installing RHadoop [rhdfs, rmr, rhbase]

    1. Download RHadoop packages from GitHub repository of Revolution Analytics: https://github.com/RevolutionAnalytics/RHadoop.

    ° rmr: [rmr-2.2.2.tar.gz]

    ° rhdfs: [rhdfs-1.6.0.tar.gz]

    ° rhbase: [rhbase-1.2.0.tar.gz]

    2. Installing packages.

    ° For rmr we use:

        ```
        R CMD INSTALL rmr-2.2.2.tar.gz
        ```

    ° For rhdfs we use:

        ```
        R CMD INSTALL rmr-2.2.2.tar.gz
        ```

    ° For rhbase we use:

        ```
        R CMD INSTALL rhbase-1.2.0.tar.gz
        ```

 To install rhbase, we need to have HBase and Zookeeper installed on our Hadoop cluster.

Understanding RHadoop examples

Once we complete the installation of RHadoop, we can test the setup by running the MapReduce job with the rmr2 and rhdfs libraries in the RHadoop sample program as follows:

```
## loading the libraries
library(rhdfs')
library('rmr2')

## initializing the RHadoop
hdfs.init()

# defining the input data
small.ints = to.dfs(1:10)

## Defining the MapReduce job
mapreduce(
```

```
# defining input parameters as small.ints hdfs object, map parameter as
function to calculate the min and max for generated random deviates.
input = small.ints,
map = function(k, v)
{
  lapply(seq_along(v), function(r){
  x <- runif(v[[r]])
  keyval(r,c(max(x),min(x)))
})})
```

After running these lines, simply pressing *Ctrl + Enter* will execute this MapReduce program. If it succeeds, the last line will appear as shown in the following screenshot:

```
packageJobJar: [/tmp/Rtmpq7v2u6/rmr-local-envd151d396330, /tmp/Rtmpq7v2u6/rmr-global-envd1512062cac,
/tmp/Rtmpq7v2u6/rmr-streaming-mapd157d0a0a23, /app/hadoop/tmp/hadoop-unjar2169767922088522341/] []
/tmp/streamjob7151352311338349586.jar tmpDir=null
13/10/15 01:33:50 INFO mapred.FileInputFormat: Total input paths to process : 1
13/10/15 01:33:51 INFO streaming.StreamJob: getLocalDirs(): [/app/hadoop/tmp/mapred/local]
13/10/15 01:33:51 INFO streaming.StreamJob: Running job: job_201310150037_0010
13/10/15 01:33:51 INFO streaming.StreamJob: To kill this job, run:
13/10/15 01:33:51 INFO streaming.StreamJob: /usr/local/hadoop/libexec/../bin/hadoop job  -
Dmapred.job.tracker=localhost:54311 -kill job_201310150037_0010
13/10/15 01:33:51 INFO streaming.StreamJob: Tracking URL: http://localhost:50030/jobdetails.jsp?
jobid=job_201310150037_0010
13/10/15 01:33:52 INFO streaming.StreamJob:  map 0%  reduce 0%
13/10/15 01:34:04 INFO streaming.StreamJob:  map 100%  reduce 0%
13/10/15 01:34:07 INFO streaming.StreamJob:  map 100%  reduce 100%
13/10/15 01:34:07 INFO streaming.StreamJob: Job complete: job 201310150037_0010
13/10/15 01:34:07 INFO streaming.StreamJob: Output: /tmp/Rtmpq7v2u6/filed1515859585
```

Where characters of that last line indicate the output location of the MapReduce job.

To read the result of the executed MapReduce job, copy the output location, as provided in the last line, and pass it to the from.dfs() function of rhdfs.

```
> output <- from.dfs('/tmp/Rtmpq7v2u6/filed1515859585')
> table_output<- do.call('rbind', lapply(output$val,"[[",2))
> table_output
            [,1]        [,2]
 [1,] 0.8125193 0.81251934
 [2,] 0.9042196 0.45699808
 [3,] 0.8646576 0.67394221
 [4,] 0.7134127 0.43075206
 [5,] 0.6928776 0.09431795
 [6,] 0.9695492 0.08021174
 [7,] 0.8968259 0.05925483
 [8,] 0.9400959 0.14835090
 [9,] 0.8650371 0.12023777
[10,] 0.7808141 0.02754461
```

Where the first column of the previous output indicates the max value, and the second one the min value.

Word count

MapReduce problem definition: This RHadoop MapReduce program is defined for identifying the frequency of all the words that are present in the provided input text files.

Also, note that this is the same MapReduce problem as we learned in the previous section about RHIPE in *Chapter 2, Writing Hadoop MapReduce Programs*.

```
wordcount = function(input,
  output = NULL,
  pattern = " "){
```

Map phase: This `map` function will read the text file line by line and split them by spaces. This map phase will assign 1 as a value to all the words that are caught by the mapper.

```
wc.map = function(., lines) {
  keyval(
  unlist(
  strsplit(
  x = lines,
  split = pattern)),
  1)}
```

Reduce phase: Reduce phase will calculate the total frequency of all the words by performing sum operations over words with the same keys.

```
wc.reduce = function(word, counts ) {
  keyval(word, sum(counts))}
```

Defining the MapReduce job: After defining the word count mapper and reducer, we need to create the `driver` method that starts the execution of MapReduce.

```
# To execute the defined Mapper and Reducer functions
# by specifying the input, output, map, reduce and input.format as
parameters.

# Syntax:
# mapreduce(input, output, input.format, map,reduce,
# combine)
```

```
mapreduce(input = input ,
  output = output,
  input.format = "text",
  map = wc.map,
  reduce = wc.reduce,
  combine = T)}
```

Executing the MapReduce job: We will execute the RHadoop MapReduce job by passing the input data location as a parameter for the wordcount function.

```
wordcount('/RHadoop/1/')
```

Exploring the wordcount output:

```
from.dfs("/tmp/RtmpRMIXzb/file2bda5e10e25f")
```

Understanding the RHadoop function reference

RHadoop has three different packages, which are in terms of HDFS, MapReduce, and HBase operations, to perform operations over the data.

Here we will see how to use the rmr and rhdfs package functions:

The hdfs package

The categorized functions are:

- Initialization
    - ° hdfs.init: This is used to initialize the rhdfs package. Its syntax is hdfs.init().
    - ° hdfs.defaults: This is used to retrieve and set the rhdfs defaults. Its syntax is hdfs.defaults().

    To retrieve the hdfs configuration defaults, refer to the following screenshot:

```
> hdfs.defaults("conf")
[1] "Java-Object{Configuration: core-default.xml, core-site.xml, mapred-default.xml,
mapred-site.xml, hdfs-default.xml, hdfs-site.xml}"
```

- File manipulation

    ° `hdfs.put`: This is used to copy files from the local filesystem to the HDFS filesystem.

    ```
    hdfs.put('/usr/local/hadoop/README.txt','/RHadoop/1/')
    ```

    ° `hdfs.copy`: This is used to copy files from the HDFS directory to the local filesystem.

    ```
    hdfs.put('/RHadoop/1/','/RHadoop/2/')
    ```

    ° `hdfs.move`: This is used to move a file from one HDFS directory to another HDFS directory.

    ```
    hdfs.move('/RHadoop/1/README.txt','/RHadoop/2/')
    ```

    ° `hdfs.rename`: This is used to rename the file stored at HDFS from R.

    ```
    hdfs.rename('/RHadoop/README.txt','/RHadoop/README1.txt')
    ```

    ° `hdfs.delete`: This is used to delete the HDFS file or directory from R.

    ```
    hdfs.delete("/RHadoop")
    ```

    ° `hdfs.rm`: This is used to delete the HDFS file or directory from R.

    ```
    hdfs.rm("/RHadoop")
    ```

    ° `hdfs.chmod`: This is used to change permissions of some files.

    ```
    hdfs.chmod('/RHadoop', permissions= '777')
    ```

- File read/write:

    ° `hdfs.file`: This is used to initialize the file to be used for read/write operation.

    ```
    f = hdfs.file("/RHadoop/2/README.
    txt","r",buffersize=104857600)
    ```

    ° `hdfs.write`: This is used to write in to the file stored at HDFS via streaming.

    ```
    f = hdfs.file("/RHadoop/2/README.
    txt","r",buffersize=104857600)
    hdfs.write(object,con,hsync=FALSE)
    ```

    ° `hdfs.close`: This is used to close the stream when a file operation is complete. It will close the stream and will not allow further file operations.

    ```
    hdfs.close(f)
    ```

- ° `hdfs.read`: This is used to read from binary files on the HDFS directory. This will use the stream for the deserialization of the data.

  f = hdfs.file("/RHadoop/2/README.txt","r",buffersize=104857600)

  m = hdfs.read(f)

  c = rawToChar(m)

  print(c)

- Directory operation:

  - ° `hdfs.dircreate` or `hdfs.mkdir`: Both these functions will be used for creating a directory over the HDFS filesystem.

    hdfs.mkdir("/RHadoop/2/")

  - ° `hdfs.rm` or `hdfs.rmr` or `hdfs.delete` - to delete the directory or file from HDFS.

    hdfs.rm("/RHadoop/2/")

- Utility:

  - ° `hdfs.ls`: This is used to list the directory from HDFS.

    Hdfs.ls('/')

```
> hdfs.ls('/')
   permission   owner      group size             modtime             file
1  drwxr-xr-x    root supergroup    0 2013-10-15 21:37              /RH
2  drwxr-xr-x    root supergroup    0 2013-10-15 01:09           /RHIPE
3  drwxrwxrwx    root supergroup    0 2013-10-15 21:38         /RHadoop
4  drwxr-xr-x hduser supergroup    0 2013-10-15 00:55             /app
5  drwxr-xr-x hduser supergroup    0 2013-06-25 14:44             /foo
6  drwxr-xr-x    root supergroup    0 2013-07-23 01:36            /hdfs
7  drwxr-xr-x hduser supergroup    0 2013-07-28 02:34             /hds
8  drwxr-xr-x hduser supergroup    0 2013-06-27 00:55            /logs
9  drwxr-xr-x    root supergroup    0 2013-07-25 02:10       /output_02
10 drwxr-xr-x hduser supergroup    0 2013-06-25 14:45             /pc
11 drwxr-xr-x hduser supergroup    0 2013-08-18 14:09 /rhadoop_examples
12 drwxrwxr-x    root supergroup    0 2013-10-15 01:33            /tmp
13 drwxr-xr-x hduser supergroup    0 2013-08-18 14:08            /user
14 drwxr-xr-x hduser supergroup    0 2013-07-25 00:59            /usr
15 drwxr-xr-x hduser supergroup    0 2013-07-25 02:17       /wordcount
```

○ hdfs.file.info: This is used to get meta information about the file stored at HDFS.

hdfs.file.info("/RHadoop")

```
> hdfs.file.info(file.path('/RHadoop'))
    perms isDir block replication owner    group size         modtime      path
1 rwxrwxrwx  TRUE     0           0  root supergroup    0 45759-03-11 06:31:51 /RHadoop
```

The rmr package

The categories of the functions are as follows:

- For storing and retrieving data:
    - ○ to.dfs: This is used to write R objects from or to the filesystem.

      small.ints = to.dfs(1:10)

    - ○ from.dfs: This is used to read the R objects from the HDFS filesystem that are in the binary encrypted format.

      from.dfs('/tmp/RtmpRMIXzb/file2bda3fa07850')

- For MapReduce:
    - ○ mapreduce: This is used for defining and executing the MapReduce job.

      mapreduce(input, output, map, reduce, combine, input.fromat, output.format, verbose)

    - ○ keyval: This is used to create and extract key-value pairs.

      keyval(key, val)

Summary

Since RHadoop is considered as matured, we will consider it while performing data analytics in further chapters. In *Chapter 5*, *Learning Data Analytics with R and Hadoop* and *Chapter 6*, *Understanding Big Data Analysis with Machine Learning*, we will dive into some Big Data analytics techniques as well as see how real world problems can be solved with RHadoop. So far we have learned how to write the MapReduce program with R and Hadoop using RHIPE and RHadoop. In the next chapter, we will see how to write the Hadoop MapReduce program with Hadoop streaming utility and also with Hadoop streaming R packages.

4
Using Hadoop Streaming with R

In the previous chapter, we learned how to integrate R and Hadoop with the help of RHIPE and RHadoop and also sample examples. In this chapter, we are going to discuss the following topics:

- Understanding the basics of Hadoop streaming
- Understanding how to run Hadoop streaming with R
- Exploring the HadoopStreaming R package

Understanding the basics of Hadoop streaming

Hadoop streaming is a Hadoop utility for running the Hadoop MapReduce job with executable scripts such as Mapper and Reducer. This is similar to the pipe operation in Linux. With this, the text input file is printed on stream (`stdin`), which is provided as an input to Mapper and the output (`stdout`) of Mapper is provided as an input to Reducer; finally, Reducer writes the output to the HDFS directory.

The main advantage of the Hadoop streaming utility is that it allows Java as well as non-Java programmed MapReduce jobs to be executed over Hadoop clusters. Also, it takes care of the progress of running MapReduce jobs. The Hadoop streaming supports the Perl, Python, PHP, R, and C++ programming languages. To run an application written in other programming languages, the developer just needs to translate the application logic into the Mapper and Reducer sections with the key and value output elements. We learned in *Chapter 2, Writing Hadoop MapReduce Programs*, that to create Hadoop MapReduce jobs we need Mapper, Reducer, and Driver as the three main components. Here, creating the driver file for running the MapReduce job is optional when we are implementing MapReduce with R and Hadoop.

This chapter is written with the intention of integrating R and Hadoop. So we will see the example of R with Hadoop streaming. Now, we will see how we can use Hadoop streaming with the R script written with Mapper and Reducer. From the following diagrams, we can identify the various components of the Hadoop streaming MapReduce job.

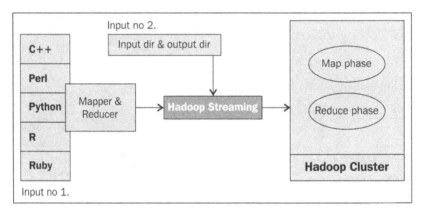

Hadoop streaming components

Now, assume we have implemented our Mapper and Reducer as `code_mapper.R` and `code_reducer.R`. We will see how we can run them in an integrated environment of R and Hadoop. This can be run with the Hadoop streaming command with various generic and streaming options.

Let's see the format of the Hadoop streaming command:

```
bin/hadoop command [generic Options] [streaming Options]
```

The following diagram shows an example of the execution of Hadoop streaming, a MapReduce job with several streaming options.

```
${HADOOP_HOME}/bin/hadoop \
              jar $HADOOP_HOME/contrib/*.jar \        ●  Line 1
              -input /app/haadoop/input \             ●  Line 2
              -output /app/haadoop/output \           ●  Line 3
              -file /usr/local/hadoop/code_mapper.R \ ●  Line 4
              -mapper code_mapper.R \                 ●  Line 5
              -file /usr/local/hadoop/code_reducer.R \ ● Line 6
              -reducer code_reducer.R                 ●  Line 7
```

Hadoop streaming command options

In the preceding image, there are about six unique important components that are required for the entire Hadoop streaming MapReduce job. All of them are streaming options except jar.

The following is a line-wise description of the preceding Hadoop streaming command:

- **Line 1**: This is used to specify the Hadoop jar files (setting up the classpath for the Hadoop jar)
- **Line 2**: This is used for specifying the input directory of HDFS
- **Line 3**: This is used for specifying the output directory of HDFS
- **Line 4**: This is used for making a file available to a local machine
- **Line 5**: This is used to define the available R file as Mapper
- **Line 6**: This is used for making a file available to a local machine
- **Line 7**: This is used to define the available R file as Reducer

The main six Hadoop streaming components of the preceding command are listed and explained as follows:

- **jar:** This option is used to run a jar with coded classes that are designed for serving the streaming functionality with Java as well as other programmed Mappers and Reducers. It's called the Hadoop streaming jar.
- **input:** This option is used for specifying the location of input dataset (stored on HDFS) to Hadoop streaming MapReduce job.

- **output:** This option is used for telling the HDFS output directory (where the output of the MapReduce job will be written) to Hadoop streaming MapReduce job.

- **file:** This option is used for copying the MapReduce resources such as Mapper, Reducer, and Combiner to computer nodes (Tasktrackers) to make it local.

- **mapper:** This option is used for identification of the executable `Mapper` file.

- **reducer:** This option is used for identification of the executable `Reducer` file.

There are other Hadoop streaming command options too, but they are optional. Let's have a look at them:

- `inputformat`: This is used to define the input data format by specifying the Java class name. By default, it's `TextInputFormat`.

- `outputformat`: This is used to define the output data format by specifying the Java class name. By default, it's `TextOutputFormat`.

- `partitioner`: This is used to include the class or file written with the code for partitioning the output as (key, value) pairs of the Mapper phase.

- `combiner`: This is used to include the class or file written with the code for reducing the Mapper output by aggregating the values of keys. Also, we can use the default combiner that will simply combine all the key attribute values before providing the Mapper's output to the Reducer.

- `cmdenv`: This option will pass the environment variable to the streaming command. For example, we can pass `R_LIBS = /your /path /to /R / libraries`.

- `inputreader`: This can be used instead of the `inputformat` class for specifying the record reader class.

- `verbose`: This is used to verbose the output.

- `numReduceTasks`: This is used to specify the number of Reducers.

- `mapdebug`: This is used to debug the script of the `Mapper` file when the Mapper task fails.

- `reducedebug`: This is used to debug the script of the `Reducer` file when the Reducer task fails.

Now, it's time to look at some generic options for the Hadoop streaming MapReduce job.

- conf: This is used to specify an application configuration file.

  ```
  -conf configuration_file
  ```

- D: This is used to define the value for a specific MapReduce or HDFS property. For example:

- -D property = value or to specify the temporary HDFS directory.

  ```
  -D dfs.temp.dir=/app/tmp/Hadoop/
  ```

  or to specify the total number of zero Reducers:

  ```
  -D mapred.reduce.tasks=0
  ```

 The -D option only works when a tool is implemented.

- fs: This is used to define the Hadoop NameNode.

  ```
  -fs localhost:port
  ```

- jt: This is used to define the Hadoop JobTracker.

  ```
  -jt localhost:port
  ```

- files: This is used to specify the large or multiple text files from HDFS.

  ```
  -files hdfs://host:port/directory/txtfile.txt
  ```

- libjars: This is used to specify the multiple jar files to be included in the classpath.

  ```
  -libjars /opt/ current/lib/a.jar, /opt/ current/lib/b.jar
  ```

- archives: This is used to specify the jar files to be unarchived on the local machine.

  ```
  -archives hdfs://host:fs_port/user/testfile.jar
  ```

Understanding how to run Hadoop streaming with R

Now, we understood what Hadoop streaming is and how it can be called with Hadoop generic as well as streaming options. Next, it's time to know how an R script can be developed and run with R. For this, we can consider a better example than a simple word count program.

The four different stages of MapReduce operations are explained here as follows:

- Understanding a MapReduce application
- Understanding how to code a MapReduce application
- Understanding how to run a MapReduce application
- Understanding how to explore the output of a MapReduce application

Understanding a MapReduce application

Problem definition: The problem is to segment a page visit by the geolocation. In this problem, we are going to consider the website `http://www.gtuadmissionhelpline.com/`, which has been developed to provide guidance to students who are looking for admission in the Gujarat Technological University. This website contains the college details of various fields such as Engineering (diploma, degree, and masters), Medical, Hotel Management, Architecture, Pharmacy, MBA, and MCA. With this MapReduce application, we will identify the fields that visitors are interested in geographically.

For example, most of the online visitors from Valsad city visit the pages of MBA colleges more often. Based on this, we can identify the mindset of Valsad students; they are highly interested in getting admissions in the MBA field. So, with this website traffic dataset, we can identify the city-wise interest levels. Now, if there are no MBA colleges in Valsad, it will be a big issue for them. They will need to relocate to other cities; this may increase the cost of their education.

By using this type of data, the Gujarat Technological University can generate informative insights for students from different cities.

Input dataset source: To perform this type of analysis, we need to have the web traffic data for that website. Google Analytics is one of the popular and free services for tracking an online visitor's metadata from the website. Google Analytics stores the web traffic data in terms of various dimensions ad metrics. We need to design a specific query to extract the dataset from Google Analytics.

Input dataset: The extracted Google Analytics dataset contains the following four data columns:

- `date`: This is the date of visit and in the form of YYYY/MM/DD.
- `country`: This is the country of the visitor.
- `city`: This is the city of the visitor.
- `pagePath`: This is the URL of a page of the website.

The head section of the input dataset is as follows:

```
$ head -5 gadata_mr.csv
20120301,India,Ahmedabad,/
20120302,India,Ahmedabad,/gtuadmissionhelpline-team
20120302,India,Mumbai,/
20120302,India,Mumbai,/merit-calculator
20120303,India,Chennai,/
```

The expected output format is shown in the following diagram:

```
[[ 1 ]]  Key ───────────────→City
    [1]  City1

[[ 2 ]] Value ──────────────→ Pagepath

[2][1]Pagepath1
[2][2]Pagepath2
[2][3]Pagepath3
[2][4]Pagepath4
```

The following is a sample output:

```
[[1]]
[1] "\"Rajkot\""

[[2]]
 [1] "\"/architecture-colleges-list\""
 [2] "\"/diplomaengineeringcollege/balaji-institute-of-engineering-technology-junagadh-\""
 [3] "\"/diplomaengineeringcollege/government-polytechnic-gandhinagar\""
 [4] "\"/gujarat-degree-engineering-college\""
 [5] "\"/me-mtech-colleges-list\""
 [6] "\"/pharmacycollege/degree-pharmacy-college-vivek-bharti-trust-junagadh\""
 [7] "\"/diploma-colleges-list\""
 [8] "\"/\""
 [9] "\"/diplomaengineeringcollege/government-polytechnic-bhuj-\""
[10] "\"/gujarat-mca-colleges-list\""
[11] "\"/d2dpharmacy/radhe-school-of-pharmacy-bio-research-institute-hirpura-\""
[12] "\"/MBA-MCA/k-b-raval-institute-of-computer-studies\""
[13] "\"/MBA-MCA/n-j-sonecha-institute-of-management-veraval\""
[14] "\"/diploma-admission-possibilities\""
[15] "\"/engineeringcollege/kankeshwari-devi-institute-of-technology-jamnagar\""
[16] "\"/engineeringcollege/noble-engineering-college-junagadh\""
[17] "\"/diplomaengineeringcollege/darshan-institute-of-engineering-technology-for-diploma-studies-rajkot\""
[18] "\"/medicalcollege/govt-dental-college-jamnagar\""
[19] "\"/d2dcollege/noble-engineering-college-junagadh\""
[20] "\"/gtud2dcalculator\""
```

Understanding how to code a MapReduce application

In this section, we will learn about the following two units of a MapReduce application:

- Mapper code
- Reducer code

Let's start with the Mapper code.

Mapper code: This R script, named `ga-mapper.R`, will take care of the Map phase of a MapReduce job.

The Mapper's job is to work on each line and extract a pair (key, value) and pass it to the Reducer to be grouped/aggregated. In this example, each line is an input to Mapper and the output `City:PagePath`. `City` is a key and `PagePath` is a value. Now Reducer can get all the page paths for a given city; hence, it can be grouped easily.

```
# To identify the type of the script, here it is RScript
#! /usr/bin/env Rscript
# To disable the warning massages to be printed
options(warn=-1)
# To initiating the connection to standard input
input <- file("stdin", "r")
```

Each line has these four fields (date, country, city, and pagePath) in the same order. We split the line by a comma. The result is a vector which has the date, country, city, and pathPath in the indexes 1,2,3, and 4 respectively.

We extract the third and fourth element for the city and pagePath respectively. Then, they will be written to the stream as key-value pairs and fed to Reducer for further processing.

```
# Running while loop until all the lines are read
while(length(currentLine <- readLines(input, n=1, warn=FALSE)) > 0) {

# Splitting the line into vectors by "," separator
  fields <- unlist(strsplit(currentLine, ","))

# Capturing the city and pagePath from fields
  city <- as.character(fields[3])
  pagepath <- as.character(fields[4])

# Printing both to the standard output
print(paste(city, pagepath,sep="\t"),stdout())



}


# Closing the connection to that input stream
close(input)
```

As soon as the output of the Mapper phase as (key, value) pairs is available to the standard output, Reducers will read the line-oriented output from stdout and convert it into final aggregated key-value pairs.

Let's see how the Mapper output format is and how the input data format of Reducer looks like.

Reducer code: This R script named ga_reducer.R will take care of the Reducer section of the MapReduce job.

As we discussed, the output of Mapper will be considered as the input for Reducer. Reducer will read these city and pagePath pairs, and combine all of the values with its respective key elements.

```
# To identify the type of the script, here it is RScript
#! /usr/bin/env Rscript


# Defining the variables with their initial values
city.key <- NA
page.value <- 0.0


# To initiating the connection to standard input
input <- file("stdin", open="r")


# Running while loop until all the lines are read
while (length(currentLine <- readLines(input, n=1)) > 0) {


# Splitting the Mapper output line into vectors by
# tab("\t") separator
  fields <- strsplit(currentLine, "\t")


# capturing key and value form the fields
# collecting the first data element from line which is city
  key <- fields[[1]][1]
# collecting the pagepath value from line
  value <- as.character(fields[[1]][2])
```

The Mapper output is written in two main fields with \t as the separator and the data line-by-line; hence, we have split the data by using \t to capture the two main attributes (key and values) from the stream input.

After collecting the key and value, the Reducer will compare it with the previously captured value. If not set previously, then set it; otherwise, combine it with the previous character value using the combine function in R and finally, print it to the HDFS output location.

```
# setting up key and values


# if block will check whether key attribute is
```

```
# initialized or not. If not initialized then it will be # assigned from
collected key attribute with value from # mapper output. This is designed
to run at initial time.
   if (is.na(city.key)) {
      city.key <- key
      page.value <- value
   }
   else {
```

```
# Once key attributes are set, then will match with the previous key
attribute value. If both of them matched then they will combined in to
one.
   if (city.key == key) {
      page.value <- c(page.value, value)


   }
   else {
```

```
# if key attributes are set already but attribute value # is other than
previous one then it will emit the store #p agepath values along with
associated key attribute value of city,

      page.value <- unique(page.value)
# printing key and value to standard output
print(list(city.key, page.value),stdout())
      city.key <- key
      page.value <- value
   }
 }
}
```

```
print(list(city.key, page.value), stdout())
```

```
# closing the connection
close(input)
```

Understanding how to run a MapReduce application

After the development of the Mapper and Reducer script with the R language, it's time to run them in the Hadoop environment. Before we execute this script, it is recommended to test them on the sample dataset with simple pipe operations.

```
$ cat gadata_sample.csv | ga_mapper.R |sort | ga_reducer.R
```

The preceding command will run the developed Mapper and Reducer scripts over a local machine. But it will run similar to the Hadoop streaming job. We need to test this for any issue that might occur at runtime or for the identification of programming or logical mistakes.

Now, we have Mapper and Reducer tested and ready to be run with the Hadoop streaming command. This Hadoop streaming operation can be executed by calling the generic `jar` command followed with the streaming command options as we learned in the *Understanding the basics of Hadoop streaming* section of this chapter. We can execute the Hadoop streaming job in the following ways:

- From a command prompt
- R or the RStudio console

The execution command with the generic and streaming command options will be the same for both the ways.

Executing a Hadoop streaming job from the command prompt

As we already learned in the section *Understanding the basics of Hadoop streaming*, the execution of Hadoop streaming MapReduce jobs developed with R can be run using the following command:

```
$ bin/hadoop jar {HADOOP_HOME}/contrib/streaming/hadoop-streaming-
1.0.3.jar
 -input /ga/gadaat_mr.csv
 -output /ga/output1
 -file /usr/local/hadoop/ga/ga_mapper.R
 -mapper ga_mapper.R
 -file /usr/local/hadoop/ga/ga_ reducer.R
 -reducer ga_reducer.R
```

Executing the Hadoop streaming job from R or an RStudio console

Being an R user, it will be more appropriate to run the Hadoop streaming job from an R console. This can be done with the `system` command:

```
system(paste("bin/hadoop jar", "{HADOOP_HOME}/contrib/streaming/hadoop-
streaming-1.0.3.jar",
 "-input /ga/gadata_mr.csv",
 "-output /ga/output2",
 "-file /usr/local/hadoop/ga/ga_mapper.R",
"-mapper ga_mapper.R",
 "-file /usr/local/hadoop/ga/ga_reducer.R",
 "-reducer ga_reducer.R"))
```

This preceding command is similar to the one that you have already used in the command prompt to execute the Hadoop streaming job with the generic options as well as the streaming options.

Understanding how to explore the output of MapReduce application

After completing the execution successfully, it's time to explore the output to check whether the generated output is important or not. The output will be generated along with two directories, `_logs` and `_SUCCESS`. `_logs` will be used for tracking all the operations as well as errors; `_SUCCESS` will be generated only on the successful completion of the MapReduce job.

Again, the commands can be fired in the following two ways:

- From a command prompt
- From an R console

Exploring an output from the command prompt

To list the generated files in the output directory, the following command will be called:

```
$ bin/hadoop dfs -cat /ga/output/part-* > temp.txt
$ head -n 40 temp.txt
```

The snapshot for checking the output is as follows:

```
hduser@ubuntu:/usr/local/hadoop$ bin/hadoop dfs -cat /ga/output/part-* > temp.txt
hduser@ubuntu:/usr/local/hadoop$ head -n 40 temp.txt
[[1]]
[1] "\"Aachen\""

[[2]]
[1] "\"/medicalcollege/m-p-shah-medical-college\""

[[1]]
[1] "\"Abbottabad\""

[[2]]
[1] "\"/merit-calculator\""

[[1]]
[1] "\"Absecon\""

[[2]]
[1] "\"/medicalcollege/gujarat-medical-education-and-research-society-gmers-medical-college\""

[[1]]
[1] "\"Abu Dhabi\""

[[2]]
 [1] "\"/architecture-college/sardar-vallabhbhai-patel-institute-of-technology-svit-\""
 [2] "\"/\""
 [3] "\"/degree-engineering-colleges-list\""
 [4] "\"/gujarat-mca-colleges-list\""
 [5] "\"/medicalcollege/s-s-agarwal-college-of-nursing-navsari\""
 [6] "\"/gtud2dcalculator\""
 [7] "\"/pharmacycollege/sardar-patel-college-of-pharmacy-for-women\""
 [8] "\"/engineeringcollege/institute-of-infrastructure-technology-research-and-management-ahmedabad\""
 [9] "\"/diploma-colleges-list\""
[10] "\"/diploma-engineering-colleges-list\""
[11] "\"/d2d-engineering-colleges-list\""
```

Exploring an output from R or an RStudio console

The same command can be used with the `system` method in the R (with RStudio) console.

```
dir <- system("bin/hadoop dfs -ls /ga/output",intern=TRUE)
out <- system("bin/hadoop dfs -cat /ga/output2/part-00000",intern=TRUE)
```

A screenshot of the preceding function is shown as follows:

Understanding basic R functions used in Hadoop MapReduce scripts

Now, we will see some basic utility functions used in Hadoop Mapper and Reducer for data processing:

- `file`: This function is used to create the connection to a file for the reading or writing operation. It is also used for reading and writing from/to `stdin` or `stdout`. This function will be used at the initiation of the Mapper and Reducer phase.

    ```
    Con <- file("stdin", "r")
    ```

- `write`: This function is used to write data to a file or standard input. It will be used after the key and value pair is set in the Mapper.

    ```
    write(paste(city,pagepath,sep="\t"),stdout())
    ```

- `print`: This function is used to write data to a file or standard input. It will be used after the key and value pair is ready in the Mapper.

    ```
    print(paste(city,pagepath,sep="\t"),stdout())
    ```

- `close`: This function can be used for closing the connection to the file after the reading or writing operation is completed. It can be used with Mapper and Reducer at the close (`conn`) end when all the processes are completed.

- stdin: This is a standard connection corresponding to the input.
  The stdin() function is a text mode connection that returns the connection
  object. This function will be used in Mapper as well as Reducer.

```
conn <- file("stdin", open="r")
```

- stdout: This is a standard connection corresponding to the output.
  The stdout() function is a text mode connection that also returns the object.
  This function will be used in Mapper as well as Reducer.

```
print(list(city.key, page.value),stdout())

## where city.key is key and page.value is value of that key
```

- sink: sink drives the R output to the connection. If there is a file or stream
  connection, the output will be returned to the file or stream. This will be used
  in Mapper and Reducer for tracking all the functional outputs as well as the
  errors.

```
sink("log.txt")
k <- 1:5
for(i in 1:k){
print(paste("value of k",k))
}sink()
unlink("log.txt")
```

Monitoring the Hadoop MapReduce job

A small syntax error in the Reducer phase leads to a failure of the MapReduce job.
After the failure of a Hadoop MapReduce job, we can track the problem from the
Hadoop MapReduce administration page, where we can get information about
running jobs as well as completed jobs.

In case of a failed job, we can see the total number of completed/failed Map and
Reduce jobs. Clicking on the failed jobs will provide the reason for the failing of
those particular number of Mappers or Reducers.

Also, we can check the real-time progress of that running MapReduce job with the
JobTracker console as shown in the following screenshot:

Hadoop job_201308010050_0007 on localhost

User: hduser
Job Name: streamjob638280349220829980.jar
Job File: hdfs://localhost:54310/app/hadoop/tmp/mapred/staging/hduser/.staging/job_201308010050_0007/job.xml
Submit Host: ubuntu
Submit Host Address: 127.0.1.1
Job-ACLs: All users are allowed
Job Setup: Successful
Status: Running
Started at: Thu Aug 01 02:57:14 PDT 2013
Running for: 2mins, 17sec
Job Cleanup: Pending

Kind	% Complete	Num Tasks	Pending	Running	Complete	Killed	Failed/Killed Task Attempts
map	100.00%	2	0	0	2	0	0 / 0
reduce	0.00%	1	0	1	0	0	0 / 0

	Counter	Map	Reduce	Total
File Input Format Counters	Bytes Read	3,454,842	0	3,454,842
Job Counters	SLOTS_MILLIS_MAPS	0	0	233,623
	Launched reduce tasks	0	0	1
	Launched map tasks	0	0	2
	Data-local map tasks	0	0	2
FileSystemCounters	HDFS_BYTES_READ	3,455,026	0	3,455,026
	FILE_BYTES_WRITTEN	2,616,420	0	2,616,420
	Map output materialized bytes	2,570,834	0	2,570,834
	Map input records	43,673	0	43,673

Monitoring Hadoop MapReduce job

Through the command, we can check the history of that particular MapReduce job by specifying its output directory with the following command:

```
$ bin/hadoop job -history /output/location
```

The following command will print the details of the MapReduce job, failed and reasons for killed up jobs.

```
$ bin/hadoop job -history all /output/location
```

The preceding command will print about the successful task and the task attempts made for each task.

Exploring the HadoopStreaming R package

HadoopStreaming is an R package developed by *David S. Rosenberg*. We can say this is a simple framework for MapReduce scripting. This also runs without Hadoop for operating data in a streaming fashion. We can consider this R package as a Hadoop MapReduce initiator. For any analyst or developer who is not able to recall the Hadoop streaming command to be passed in the command prompt, this package will be helpful to quickly run the Hadoop MapReduce job.

The three main features of this package are as follows:

- Chunkwise data reading: The package allows chunkwise data reading and writing for Hadoop streaming. This feature will overcome memory issues.

- Supports various data formats: The package allows the reading and writing of data in three different data formats.

- Robust utility for the Hadoop streaming command: The package also allows users to specify the command-line argument for Hadoop streaming.

This package is mainly designed with three functions for reading the data efficiently:

- `hsTableReader`

- `hsKeyValReader`

- `hsLineReader`

Now, let's understand these functions and their use cases. After that we will understand these functions with the help of the word count MapReduce job.

Understanding the hsTableReader function

The `hsTableReader` function is designed for reading data in the table format. This function assumes that there is an input connection established with the file, so it will retrieve the entire row. It assumes that all the rows with the same keys are stored consecutively in the input file.

As the Hadoop streaming job guarantees that the output rows of Mappers will be sorted before providing to the reducers, there is no need to use the `sort` function in a Hadoop streaming MapReduce job. When we are not running this over Hadoop, we explicitly need to call the `sort` function after the `Mapper` function gets execute.

Defining a function of `hsTableReader`:

```
hsTableReader(file="", cols='character',
  chunkSize=-1, FUN=print,
  ignoreKey=TRUE, singleKey=TRUE, skip=0,
  sep='\t', keyCol='key',
  FUN=NULL, ,carryMemLimit=512e6,
  carryMaxRows=Inf,
  stringsAsFactors=FALSE)
```

The terms in the preceding code are as follows:

- `file`: This is a connection object, stream, or string.
- `chunkSize`: This indicates the maximum number of lines to be read at a time by the function. `-1` means all the lines at a time.
- `cols`: This means a list of column names as "what" argument to scan.
- `skip`: This is used to skip the first n data rows.
- `FUN`: This function will use the data entered by the user.
- `carryMemLimit`: This indicates the maximum memory limit for the values of a single key.
- `carryMaxRows`: This indicates the maximum rows to be considered or read from the file.
- `stringsAsFactors`: This defines whether the strings are converted to factors or not (TRUE or FALSE).

For example, data in file:

```
# Loading libraries
Library("HadoopStreaming")
# Input data String with collection of key and values
str <- "
  key1\t1.91\nkey1\t2.1\nkey1\t20.2\nkey1\t3.2\
  nkey2\t1.2\nkey2\t10\nkey3\t2.5\nkey3\t2.1\nkey4\t1.2\n"

  cat(str)
```

The output for the preceding code is as shown in the following screenshot:

```
> str <- "key1\t1.91\nkey1\t2.1\nkey1\t20.2\nkey1\t3.2\nkey2\t1.2\nkey2\t10\nkey3\t2.5\nkey3\t2.1\nkey4\t1.2\n
> cat(str)
key1 1.91
key1 2.1
key1 20.2
key1 3.2
key2 1.2
key2 10
key3 2.5
key3 2.1
key4 1.2
```

The data read by `hsTableReader` is as follows:

```
# A list of column names, as'what' arg to scan
cols = list(key='',val=0)


# To make a text connection
con <- textConnection(str, open = "r")


# To read the data with chunksize 3
hsTableReader(con,cols,chunkSize=3,FUN=print,ignoreKey=TRUE)
```

The output for the preceding code is as shown in the following screenshot:

```
> hsTableReader(con,cols,chunkSize=3,FUN=print,ignoreKey=TRUE)
    key    val
1 key1   1.91
2 key1   2.10
3 key1  20.20
    key  val
1 key1   3.2
2 key2   1.2
3 key2  10.0
    key val
1 key3 2.5
2 key3 2.1
3 key4 1.2
```

Understanding the hsKeyValReader function

The `hsKeyValReader` function is designed for reading the data available in the key-value pair format. This function also uses `chunkSize` for defining the number of lines to be read at a time, and each line consists of a key string and a value string.

```
hsKeyValReader(file = "", chunkSize = -1, skip = 0, sep = "\t",FUN =
    function(k, v) cat(paste(k, v))
```

The terms of this function are similar to `hsTablereader()`.

Example:

```
# Function for reading chunkwise dataset
printkeyval <- function(k,v) {
  cat('A chunk:\n')
  cat(paste(k,v,sep=': '),sep='\n')
}

str <- "key1\tval1\nkey2\tval2\nkey3\tval3\n"

con <- textConnection(str, open = "r")

hsKeyValReader(con, chunkSize=1, FUN=printFn)
```

The output for the preceding code is as shown in the following screenshot:

```
> hsKeyValReader(con,chunkSize=1,FUN=printFn)
A chunk:
key1: val1
A chunk:
key2: val2
A chunk:
key3: val3
```

Understanding the hsLineReader function

The hsLineReader function is designed for reading the entire line as a string without performing the data-parsing operation. It repeatedly reads the chunkSize lines of data from the file and passes a character vector of these strings to FUN.

```
hsLineReader(file = "", chunkSize = 3, skip = 0, FUN = function(x)
  cat(x, sep = "\n"))
```

The terms of this function are similar to hsTablereader().

Example:

```
str <- " This is HadoopStreaming!!\n here are,\n examples for chunk
dataset!!\n in R\n   ?"

#  For defining the string as data source
con <- textConnection(str, open = "r")

# read from the con object
hsLineReader(con,chunkSize=2,FUN=print)
```

The output for the preceding code is as shown in the following screenshot:

```
> hsLineReader(con,chunkSize=2,FUN=print)
[1] "This is HadoopStreaming!!" " here are,"
[1] " exampels for chunk dataset!!" " in R"
[1] "  ?"
```

You can get more information on these methods as well as other existing methods at `http://cran.r-project.org/web/packages/HadoopStreaming/HadoopStreaming.pdf`.

Now, we will implement the above data-reading methods with the Hadoop MapReduce program to be run over Hadoop. In some of the cases, the key-values pairs or data rows will not be fed in the machine memory; so reading that data chunk wise will be more appropriate than improving the machine configuration.

Problem definition:

Hadoop word count: As we already know what a word count application is, we will implement the above given methods with the concept of word count. This R script has been reproduced here from the HadoopStreaming R package, which can be downloaded along with the HadoopStreaming R library distribution as the sample code.

Input dataset: This has been taken from *Chapter 1* of *Anna Karenina* (novel) by the Russian writer *Leo Tolstoy*.

R script: This section contains the code of the Mapper, Reducer, and the rest of the configuration parameters.

File: `hsWordCnt.R`

```
## Loading the library
library(HadoopStreaming)


## Additional command line arguments for this script (rest are
  default in hsCmdLineArgs)
spec = c('printDone','D',0,"logical","A flag to write DONE at the
  end.",FALSE)


opts = hsCmdLineArgs(spec, openConnections=T)


if (!opts$set) {
```

```r
  quit(status=0)
}


# Defining the Mapper columns names
mapperOutCols = c('word','cnt')


# Defining the Reducer columns names
reducerOutCols = c('word','cnt')


# printing the column header for Mapper output
if (opts$mapcols) {
  cat( paste(mapperOutCols,collapse=opts$outsep),'\n',
    file=opts$outcon )
}



# Printing the column header for Reducer output
if (opts$reducecols) {
  cat( paste(reducerOutCols,collapse=opts$outsep),'\n',
    file=opts$outcon )
}


## For running the Mapper
if (opts$mapper) {
  mapper <- function(d) {
    words <- strsplit(paste(d,collapse=' '),'[[:punct:][:space:]]+')[[1]]
# split on punctuation and spaces
    words <- words[!(words=='')]   # get rid of empty words caused by
whitespace at beginning of lines
    df = data.frame(word=words)
    df[,'cnt']=1


# For writing the output in the form of key-value table format
hsWriteTable(df[,mapperOutCols],file=opts$outcon,sep=opts$outsep)
  }



## For chunk wise reading the Mapper output, to be fed to Reducer hsLi
neReader(opts$incon,chunkSize=opts$chunksize,FUN=mapper)
```

```
## For running the Reducer
} else if (opts$reducer) {

  reducer <- function(d) {
    cat(d[1,'word'],sum(d$cnt),'\n',sep=opts$outsep)
  }
  cols=list(word='',cnt=0)  # define the column names and types
(''-->string 0-->numeric)
  hsTableReader(opts$incon,cols,chunkSize=opts$chunksize,skip=opts$skip,s
ep=opts$insep,keyCol='word',singleKey=T, ignoreKey= F, FUN=reducer)
  if (opts$printDone) {
    cat("DONE\n");
  }
}


# For closing the connection corresponding to input
if (!is.na(opts$infile)) {
  close(opts$incon)
}


# For closing the connection corresponding to input
if (!is.na(opts$outfile)) {
  close(opts$outcon)
}
```

Running a Hadoop streaming job

Since this is a Hadoop streaming job, it will run same as the executed previous
example of a Hadoop streaming job. For this example, we will use a shell script to
execute the runHadoop.sh file to run Hadoop streaming.

Setting up the system environment variable:

```
#! /usr/bin/env bash
HADOOP="$HADOOP_HOME/bin/hadoop"    # Hadoop command

HADOOPSTREAMING="$HADOOP jar
$HADOOP_HOME/contrib/streaming/hadoop-streaming-1.0.3.jar" # change
version number as appropriate
```

```
RLIBPATH=/usr/local/lib/R/site-library  # can specify additional R
Library paths here
```

Setting up the MapReduce job parameters:

```
INPUTFILE="anna.txt"
HFSINPUTDIR="/HadoopStreaming"
OUTDIR="/HadoopStreamingRpkg_output"


RFILE=" home/hduser/Desktop/HadoopStreaming/inst/wordCntDemo/
hsWordCnt.R"
#LOCALOUT="/home/hduser/Desktop/HadoopStreaming/inst/wordCntDemo/
annaWordCnts.out"
# Put the file into the Hadoop file system
#$HADOOP fs -put $INPUTFILE $HFSINPUTDIR
```

Removing the existing output directory:

```
# Remove the directory if already exists (otherwise, won't run)
#$HADOOP fs -rmr $OUTDIR
```

Designing the Hadoop MapReduce command with generic and streaming options:

```
MAPARGS="--mapper"
REDARGS="--reducer"
JOBARGS="-cmdenv R_LIBS=$RLIBPATH" # numReduceTasks 0
# echo $HADOOPSTREAMING -cmdenv R_LIBS=$RLIBPATH  -input
$HFSINPUTDIR/$INPUTFILE -output $OUTDIR -mapper "$RFILE $MAPARGS"
-reducer "$RFILE $REDARGS" -file $RFILE


$HADOOPSTREAMING $JOBARGS   -input $HFSINPUTDIR/$INPUTFILE -output
$OUTDIR -mapper "$RFILE $MAPARGS" -reducer "$RFILE $REDARGS" -file $RFILE
```

Extracting the output from HDFS to the local directory:

```
# Extract output
./$RFILE --reducecols > $LOCALOUT
$HADOOP fs -cat $OUTDIR/part* >> $LOCALOUT
```

Executing the Hadoop streaming job

We can now execute the Hadoop streaming job by executing the command, `runHadoop.sh`. To execute this, we need to set the user permission.

```
sudo chmod +x runHadoop.sh
```

Executing via the following command:

```
./runHadoop.sh
```

Finally, it will execute the whole Hadoop streaming job and then copy the output to the local directory.

Summary

We have learned most of the ways to integrate R and Hadoop for performing data operations. In the next chapter, we will learn about the data analytics cycle for solving real world data analytics problems with the help of R and Hadoop.

5
Learning Data Analytics with R and Hadoop

In the previous chapters we learned about the installation, configuration, and integration of R and Hadoop.

In this chapter, we will learn how to perform data analytics operations over an integrated R and Hadoop environment. Since this chapter is designed for data analytics, we will understand this with an effective data analytics cycle.

In this chapter we will learn about:

- Understanding the data analytics project life cycle
- Understanding data analytics problems

Understanding the data analytics project life cycle

While dealing with the data analytics projects, there are some fixed tasks that should be followed to get the expected output. So here we are going to build a data analytics project cycle, which will be a set of standard data-driven processes to lead data to insights effectively. The defined data analytics processes of a project life cycle should be followed by sequences for effectively achieving the goal using input datasets. This data analytics process may include identifying the data analytics problems, designing, and collecting datasets, data analytics, and data visualization.

The data analytics project life cycle stages are seen in the following diagram:

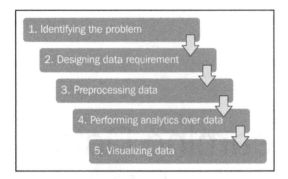

Let's get some perspective on these stages for performing data analytics.

Identifying the problem

Today, business analytics trends change by performing data analytics over web datasets for growing business. Since their data size is increasing gradually day by day, their analytical application needs to be scalable for collecting insights from their datasets.

With the help of web analytics, we can solve the business analytics problems. Let's assume that we have a large e-commerce website, and we want to know how to increase the business. We can identify the important pages of our website by categorizing them as per popularity into high, medium, and low. Based on these popular pages, their types, their traffic sources, and their content, we will be able to decide the roadmap to improve business by improving web traffic, as well as content.

Designing data requirement

To perform the data analytics for a specific problem, it needs datasets from related domains. Based on the domain and problem specification, the data source can be decided and based on the problem definition; the data attributes of these datasets can be defined.

For example, if we are going to perform social media analytics (problem specification), we use the data source as Facebook or Twitter. For identifying the user characteristics, we need user profile information, likes, and posts as data attributes.

Preprocessing data

In data analytics, we do not use the same data sources, data attributes, data tools, and algorithms all the time as all of them will not use data in the same format. This leads to the performance of data operations, such as data cleansing, data aggregation, data augmentation, data sorting, and data formatting, to provide the data in a supported format to all the data tools as well as algorithms that will be used in the data analytics.

In simple terms, preprocessing is used to perform data operation to translate data into a fixed data format before providing data to algorithms or tools. The data analytics process will then be initiated with this formatted data as the input.

In case of Big Data, the datasets need to be formatted and uploaded to **Hadoop Distributed File System** (**HDFS**) and used further by various nodes with Mappers and Reducers in Hadoop clusters.

Performing analytics over data

After data is available in the required format for data analytics algorithms, data analytics operations will be performed. The data analytics operations are performed for discovering meaningful information from data to take better decisions towards business with data mining concepts. It may either use descriptive or predictive analytics for business intelligence.

Analytics can be performed with various machine learning as well as custom algorithmic concepts, such as regression, classification, clustering, and model-based recommendation. For Big Data, the same algorithms can be translated to MapReduce algorithms for running them on Hadoop clusters by translating their data analytics logic to the MapReduce job which is to be run over Hadoop clusters. These models need to be further evaluated as well as improved by various evaluation stages of machine learning concepts. Improved or optimized algorithms can provide better insights.

Visualizing data

Data visualization is used for displaying the output of data analytics. Visualization is an interactive way to represent the data insights. This can be done with various data visualization softwares as well as R packages. R has a variety of packages for the visualization of datasets. They are as follows:

- `ggplot2`: This is an implementation of the Grammar of Graphics by *Dr. Hadley Wickham* (http://had.co.nz/). For more information refer http://cran.r-project.org/web/packages/ggplot2/.

- `rCharts`: This is an R package to create, customize, and publish interactive JavaScript visualizations from R by using a familiar lattice-style plotting interface by *Markus Gesmann* and *Diego de Castillo*. For more information refer http://ramnathv.github.io/rCharts/.

Some popular examples of visualization with R are as follows:

- **Plots for facet scales** (`ggplot`): The following figure shows the comparison of males and females with different measures; namely, education, income, life expectancy, and literacy, using `ggplot`:

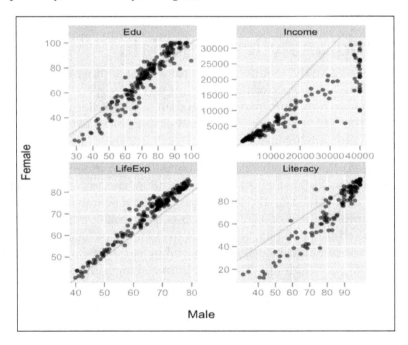

- **Dashboard charts**: This is an `rCharts` type. Using this we can build interactive animated dashboards with R.

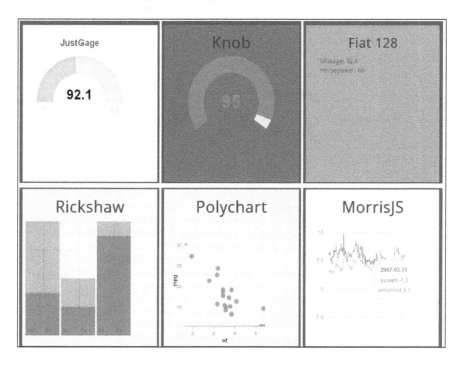

Understanding data analytics problems

In this section, we have included three practical data analytics problems with various stages of data-driven activity with R and Hadoop technologies. These data analytics problem definitions are designed such that readers can understand how Big Data analytics can be done with the analytical power of functions, packages of R, and the computational powers of Hadoop.

The data analytics problem definitions are as follows:

- Exploring the categorization of web pages
- Computing the frequency of changes in the stock market
- Predicting the sale price of a blue book for bulldozers (case study)

Exploring web pages categorization

This data analytics problem is designed to identify the category of a web page of a website, which may categorized popularity wise as high, medium, or low (regular), based on the visit count of the pages. While designing the data requirement stage of the data analytics life cycle, we will see how to collect these types of data from **Google Analytics**.

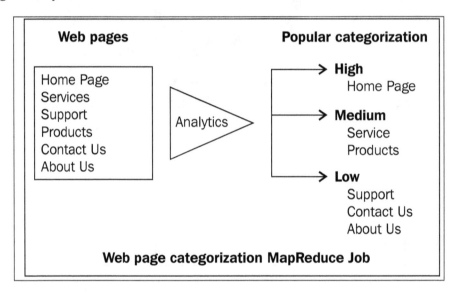

Identifying the problem

As this is a web analytics problem, the goal of the problem is to identify the importance of web pages designed for websites. Based on this information, the content, design, or visits of the lower popular pages can be improved or increased.

Designing data requirement

In this section, we will be working with data requirement as well as data collection for this data analytics problem. First let's see how the requirement for data can be achieved for this problem.

Since this is a web analytics problem, we will use Google Analytics data source. To retrieve this data from Google Analytics, we need to have an existent Google Analytics account with web traffic data stored on it. To increase the popularity, we will require the visits information of all of the web pages. Also, there are many other attributes available in Google Analytics with respect to dimensions and metrics.

Understanding the required Google Analytics data attributes

The header format of the dataset to be extracted from Google Analytics is as follows:

```
date, source, pageTitle, pagePath
```

- `date`: This is the date of the day when the web page was visited
- `source`: This is the referral to the web page
- `pageTitle`: This is the title of the web page
- `pagePath`: This is the URL of the web page

Collecting data

As we are going to extract the data from Google Analytics, we need to use `RGoogleAnalytics`, which is an R library for extracting Google Analytics datasets within R. To extract data, you need this plugin to be installed in R. Then you will be able to use its functions.

The following is the code for the extraction process from Google Analytics:

```
# Loading the RGoogleAnalytics library
require("RGoogleAnalyics")

# Step 1. Authorize your account and paste the access_token
query <- QueryBuilder()
access_token <- query$authorize()

# Step 2. Create a new Google Analytics API object
ga <- RGoogleAnalytics()

# To retrieve profiles from Google Analytics
ga.profiles <- ga$GetProfileData(access_token)

# List the GA profiles
ga.profiles

# Step 3. Setting up the input parameters
profile <- ga.profiles$id[3]
startdate <- "2010-01-08"
enddate <- "2013-08-23"
dimension <- "ga:date,ga:source,ga:pageTitle,ga:pagePath"
metric <- "ga:visits"
sort <- "ga:visits"
maxresults <- 100099
```

```
# Step 4. Build the query string, use the profile by setting its index
value
query$Init(start.date = startdate,
          end.date = enddate,
          dimensions = dimension,
          metrics = metric,

          max.results = maxresults,
          table.id = paste("ga:",profile,sep="",collapse=","),
          access_token=access_token)

# Step 5. Make a request to get the data from the API
ga.data <- ga$GetReportData(query)

# Look at the returned data
head(ga.data)
write.csv(ga.data,"webpages.csv", row.names=FALSE)
```

The preceding file will be available with the chapter contents for download.

Preprocessing data

Now, we have the raw data for Google Analytics available in a CSV file. We need to process this data before providing it to the MapReduce algorithm.

There are two main changes that need to be performed into the dataset:

- Query parameters needs to be removed from the column pagePath as follows:

```
pagePath <- as.character(data$pagePath)
pagePath <- strsplit(pagePath,"\\?")
pagePath <- do.call("rbind", pagePath)
pagePath <- pagePath [,1]
```

- The new CSV file needs to be created as follows:

```
data   <- data.frame(source=data$source, pagePath=d,visits =)
write.csv(data, "webpages_mapreduce.csv" , row.names=FALSE)
```

Performing analytics over data

To perform the categorization over website pages, we will build and run the MapReduce algorithm with R and Hadoop integration. As already discussed in the *Chapter 2, Writing Hadoop MapReduce Programs*, sometimes we need to use multiple Mappers and Reducers for performing data analytics; this means using the chained MapReduce jobs.

In case of chaining MapReduce jobs, multiple Mappers and Reducers can communicate in such a way that the output of the first job will be assigned to the second job as input. The MapReduce execution sequence is described in the following diagram:

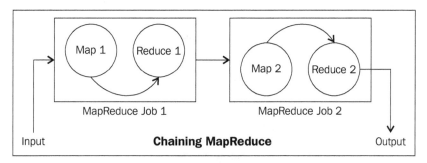

Chaining MapReduce

Now let's start with the programming task to perform analytics:

1. Initialize by setting Hadoop variables and loading the `rmr2` and `rhdfs` packages of the RHadoop libraries:

    ```
    # setting up the Hadoop variables need by RHadoop
    Sys.setenv(HADOOP_HOME="/usr/local/hadoop/")
    Sys.setenv(HADOOP_CMD="/usr/local/hadoop/bin/hadoop")

    # Loading the RHadoop libraries rmr2 and rhdfs
    library(rmr2)
    library(rhdfs)

    # To initializing hdfs
    hdfs.init()
    ```

2. Upload the datasets to HDFS:

    ```
    # First uploading the data to R console,
    webpages <- read.csv("/home/vigs/Downloads/webpages_mapreduce.
    csv")

    # saving R file object to HDFS,
    webpages.hdfs <- to.dfs(webpages)
    ```

Now we will see the development of Hadoop MapReduce job 1 for these analytics. We will divide this job into Mapper and Reducer. Since, there are two MapReduce jobs, there will be two Mappers and Reducers. Also note that here we need to create only one file for both the jobs with all Mappers and Reducers. Mapper and Reducer will be established by defining their separate functions.

Let's see MapReduce job 1.

- **Mapper 1**: The code for this is as follows:

```
mapper1 <- function(k,v) {

    # To storing pagePath column data in to key object
    key <- v[2]

    # To store visits column data into val object
    Val <- v[3]

    # emitting key and value for each row
    keyval(key, val)
}
totalvisits <- sum(webpages$visits)
```

- **Reducer 1**: The code for this is as follows:

```
reducer1 <- function(k,v) {

    # Calculating percentage visits for the specific URL
    per <- (sum(v)/totalvisits)*100
    # Identify the category of URL
    if (per <33 )
    {
val <- "low"
}
    if (per >33 && per < 67)
    {
val <- "medium"
}
    if (per > 67)
    {
val <- "high"
}

    # emitting key and values
    keyval(k, val)

}
```

- **Output of MapReduce job 1**: The intermediate output for the information is shown in the following screenshot:

```
$key
                                                 pagePath
1                                                        /
2                                           /abranch.php
3                                           /admission/
4                                           /admissioN/
5           /admission/diplomaadmissionpossibilities1.php
6                                        /advertisewithus
7                               /bindingcollegedetails.php
8                               /bindingmpharmcollege.php
9                    /engineering-admission-possibilities
10                              /gtuadmissionhelpline-team
11                    /gujarat-degree-engineering-college
12          /MBA-MCA/aes-institute-of-computer-studies
13 /medicalcollege/s-s-agarwal-college-of-nursing-navsari
14                                          /meritcalc.php
15                                        /merit-calculator
16                                 /new_mba_college_list.php
17                                         /newmecollege.php
18                                  /newmpharmcollege.php
19                                          /ourteam.php
20                                               /search
21                                            /search2.php
22                                            /search3.php
23                                             /search.php

$val
 [1] "high" "low"  "low"  "low"  "low"  "low"  "low"  "low"  "low"  "low"  "low"  "low"  "low"  "low"  "low"  "low"
[17] "low"  "low"  "low"  "low"  "low"  "low"  "low"
```

The output in the preceding screenshot is only for information about the output of this MapReduce job 1. This can be considered an intermediate output where only 100 data rows have been considered from the whole dataset for providing output. In these rows, 23 URLs are unique; so the output has provided 23 URLs.

Let's see Hadoop MapReduce job 2:

- **Mapper 2**: The code for this is as follows:

```
#Mapper:
mapper2 <- function(k, v) {

# Reversing key and values and emitting them
 keyval(v,k)

}
```

- **Reducer 2**: The code for this is as follows:

```
key <- NA
val <- NULL
# Reducer:
reducer2   <-   function(k, v) {


# for checking whether key-values are already assigned or not.
 if(is.na(key)) {
 key <- k
 val <- v
   } else {
     if(key==k) {
 val <- c(val,v)
   } else{
     key <- k
     val <- v
     }
   }
# emitting key and list of values

keyval(key,list(val))

 }
```

> Before executing the MapReduce job, please start all the Hadoop
> daemons and check the HDFS connection via the hdfs.init() method.
> If your Hadoop daemons have not been started, you can start them by
> $hduser@ubuntu :~ $HADOOP_HOME/bin/start-all.sh.

Once we are ready with the logic of the Mapper and Reducer, MapReduce jobs
can be executed by the MapReduce method of the rmr2 package. Here we have
developed multiple MapReduce jobs, so we need to call the mapreduce function
within the mapreduce function with the required parameters.

The command for calling a chained MapReduce job is seen in the following figure:

```
# executing Hadoop MapReduce
output <- mapreduce(input=mapreduce(input=webpages.values,
                                    map = mapper1,
                                    reduce = reducer1),
                                    map = mapper2,
                                    reduce = reducer2,
                                    combine = TRUE)
```

The following is the command for retrieving the generated output from HDFS:

`from.dfs(output)`

While executing Hadoop MapReduce, the execution log output will be printed over the terminal for the purpose of monitoring. We will understand MapReduce job 1 and MapReduce job 2 by separating them into different parts.

The details for MapReduce job 1 is as follows:

- **Tracking the MapReduce job metadata**: With this initial portion of log, we can identify the metadata for the Hadoop MapReduce job. We can also track the job status with the web browser by calling the given `Tracking URL`.

```
packageJobJar: [/tmp/Rtmpn7tKAv/rmr-local-enve056d43a14e, /tmp/Rtmpn7tKAv/rmr-global-enve05d2d95c,
/tmp/Rtmpn7tKAv/rmr-streaming-mape055f73cd8c, /tmp/Rtmpn7tKAv/rmr-streaming-reducee0529eb924e, /app/hadoop/tmp/hadoop-
unjar6101512165582043075/] [] /tmp/streamjob5358198509362391792.jar tmpDir=null
13/10/24 13:45:21 INFO mapred.FileInputFormat: Total input paths to process : 1
13/10/24 13:45:22 INFO streaming.StreamJob: getLocalDirs(): [/app/hadoop/tmp/mapred/local]
13/10/24 13:45:22 INFO streaming.StreamJob: Running job: job_201310241342_0001
13/10/24 13:45:22 INFO streaming.StreamJob: To kill this job, run:
13/10/24 13:45:22 INFO streaming.StreamJob: /usr/local/hadoop/libexec/../bin/hadoop job  -
Dmapred.job.tracker=localhost:54311 -kill job_201310241342_0001
13/10/24 13:45:22 INFO streaming.StreamJob: Tracking URL: http://localhost:50030/jobdetails.jsp?
jobid=job_201310241342_0001
```

- **Tracking status of Mapper and Reducer tasks**: With this portion of log, we can monitor the status of the Mapper or Reducer task being run on Hadoop cluster to get details such as whether it was a success or a failure.

```
13/10/24 13:45:23 INFO streaming.StreamJob:  map 0%  reduce 0%
13/10/24 13:46:02 INFO streaming.StreamJob:  map 50%  reduce 0%
13/10/24 13:46:11 INFO streaming.StreamJob:  map 100%  reduce 0%
13/10/24 13:46:20 INFO streaming.StreamJob:  map 100%  reduce 17%
13/10/24 13:46:23 INFO streaming.StreamJob:  map 100%  reduce 100%
13/10/24 13:46:35 INFO streaming.StreamJob: Job complete: job_201310241342_0001
```

- **Tracking HDFS output location**: Once the MapReduce job is completed, its output location will be displayed at the end of logs.

```
13/10/24 13:46:35 INFO streaming.StreamJob: Output: /tmp/Rtmpn7tKAv/filee05467211b
```

For MapReduce job 2.

- **Tracking the MapReduce job metadata**: With this initial portion of log, we can identify the metadata for the Hadoop MapReduce job. We can also track the job status with the web browser by calling the given Tracking URL.

```
packageJobJar: [/tmp/Rtmpn7tKAv/rmr-local-enve055fb43a38, /tmp/Rtmpn7tKAv/rmr-global-enve0549c1f8a5,
/tmp/Rtmpn7tKAv/rmr-streaming-mape052bf9ab69, /tmp/Rtmpn7tKAv/rmr-streaming-reducee0552cf3c79, /tmp/Rtmpn7tKAv/rmr-
streaming-combinee0534783636, /app/hadoop/tmp/hadoop-unjar2866287784631685861/] []
/tmp/streamjob8204691495163848860.jar tmpDir=null
13/10/24 13:46:38 INFO mapred.FileInputFormat: Total input paths to process : 1
13/10/24 13:46:38 INFO streaming.StreamJob: getLocalDirs(): [/app/hadoop/tmp/mapred/local]
13/10/24 13:46:38 INFO streaming.StreamJob: Running job: job_201310241342_0002
13/10/24 13:46:38 INFO streaming.StreamJob: To kill this job, run:
13/10/24 13:46:38 INFO streaming.StreamJob: /usr/local/hadoop/libexec/../bin/hadoop job  -
Dmapred.job.tracker=localhost:54311 -kill job_201310241342_0002
13/10/24 13:46:38 INFO streaming.StreamJob: Tracking URL: http://localhost:50030/jobdetails.jsp?
jobid=job_201310241342_0002
```

- **Tracking status of the Mapper and Reducer tasks**: With this portion of log, we can monitor the status of the Mapper or Reducer tasks being run on the Hadoop cluster to get the details such as whether it was successful or failed.

```
13/10/24 13:46:39 INFO streaming.StreamJob:  map 0%  reduce 0%
13/10/24 13:46:56 INFO streaming.StreamJob:  map 4%  reduce 0%
13/10/24 13:46:59 INFO streaming.StreamJob:  map 9%  reduce 0%
13/10/24 13:47:08 INFO streaming.StreamJob:  map 55%  reduce 0%
13/10/24 13:47:15 INFO streaming.StreamJob:  map 100%  reduce 0%
13/10/24 13:47:30 INFO streaming.StreamJob:  map 100%  reduce 33%
13/10/24 13:47:36 INFO streaming.StreamJob:  map 100%  reduce 100%
13/10/24 13:47:42 INFO streaming.StreamJob: Job complete: job_201310241342_0002
```

- **Tracking HDFS output location**: Once the MapReduce job is completed, its output location will be displayed at the end of the logs.

```
13/10/24 13:47:42 INFO streaming.StreamJob: Output: /tmp/Rtmpn7tKAv/filee05767f2
```

The output of this chained MapReduce job is stored at an HDFS location, which can be retrieved by the command:

```
from.dfs(output)
```

The response to the preceding command is shown in the following figure (output only for the top 1000 rows of the dataset):

```
$key
[1] "low"   "high"

$val
$val[[1]]
$val[[1]][[1]]
                                                pagePath
1    /medicalcollege/s-s-agarwal-college-of-nursing-navsari
2                                           /meritcalc.php
3                                         /merit-calculator
4                                  /new_mba_college_list.php
5                                         /newmecollege.php
6                                      /newmpharmcollege.php
7                                            /ourteam.php
8                                                /search
9                                           /search2.php
10                                          /search3.php
11                                           /search.php


$val[[1]][[2]]
                                                pagePath
1                                            /abranch.php
2                                             /admission/
3                                             /admissioN/
4    /admission/diplomaadmissionpossibilities1.php
5                                          /advertisewithus
6                                  /bindingcollegedetails.php
7                                     /bindingmpharmcollege.php
8                        /engineering-admission-possibilities
9                                /gtuadmissionhelpline-team
10                       /gujarat-degree-engineering-college
11       /MBA-MCA/aes-institute-of-computer-studies


$val[[2]]
$val[[2]][[1]]
    pagePath
12        /
--             ,
```

Visualizing data

We collected the web page categorization output using the three categories. I think the best thing we can do is simply list the URLs. But if we have more information, such as sources, we can represent the web pages as nodes of a graph, colored by popularity with directed edges when users follow the links. This can lead to more informative insights.

Computing the frequency of stock market change

This data analytics MapReduce problem is designed for calculating the frequency of stock market changes.

Identifying the problem

Since this is a typical stock market data analytics problem, it will calculate the frequency of past changes for one particular symbol of the stock market, such as a **Fourier Transformation**. Based on this information, the investor can get more insights on changes for different time periods. So the goal of this analytics is to calculate the frequencies of percentage change.

Yahoo finance data for symbol BP						
Date	Open	High	Low	Close	Volume	Adj Close
2013-08-23	41.16	41.54	41.11	41.51	4117400	41.51
2013-08-22	40.82	40.99	40.75	40.91	2808300	40.91
2013-08-21	40.84	40.89	40.51	40.53	4296800	40.53
2013-08-20	41.02	40.90	40.90	4354200	40.90	
2013-08-19	41.29	41.35	41.05	41.10	3633800	41.10

Change	Frequency
-0.1	20
0.3	2
0.8	1
1.0	22
1.9	12

Change frequency calculation for Yahoo Finance data

Designing data requirement

For this stock market analytics, we will use Yahoo! Finance as the input dataset. We need to retrieve the specific symbol's stock information. To retrieve this data, we will use the Yahoo! API with the following parameters:

- From month
- From day
- From year
- To month
- To day
- To year
- Symbol

 For more information on this API, visit http://developer.yahoo.com/finance/.

Preprocessing data

To perform the analytics over the extracted dataset, we will use R to fire the following command:

```
stock_BP <- read.csv("http://ichart.finance.yahoo.com/table.csv?s=BP")
```

Or you can also download via the terminal:

```
wget http://ichart.finance.yahoo.com/table.csv?s=BP
#exporting to csv file

write.csv(stock_BP,"table.csv", row.names=FALSE)
```

Then upload it to HDFS by creating a specific Hadoop directory for this:

```
# creating /stock directory in hdfs
bin/hadoop dfs -mkdir /stock

# uploading table.csv to hdfs in /stock directory
bin/hadoop dfs -put /home/Vignesh/downloads/table.csv /stock/
```

Performing analytics over data

To perform the data analytics operations, we will use streaming with R and Hadoop (without the `HadoopStreaming` package). So, the development of this MapReduce job can be done without any RHadoop integrated library/package.

In this MapReduce job, we have defined Map and Reduce in different R files to be provided to the Hadoop streaming function.

- **Mapper**: `stock_mapper.R`

```
#! /usr/bin/env/Rscript
# To disable the warnings
options(warn=-1)
# To take input the data from streaming
input <- file("stdin", "r")


# To reading the each lines of documents till the end
while(length(currentLine <-readLines(input, n=1, warn=FALSE)) > 0)
{

# To split the line by "," seperator
fields <- unlist(strsplit(currentLine, ","))

# Capturing open column value
 open <- as.double(fields[2])

# Capturing close columns value
 close <- as.double(fields[5])

# Calculating the difference of close and open attribute
   change <- (close-open)

# emitting change as key and value as 1
write(paste(change, 1, sep="\t"), stdout())
}

close(input)
```

- **Reducer:** `stock_reducer.R`

```
#! /usr/bin/env Rscript
stock.key <- NA
stock.val <- 0.0

conn <- file("stdin", open="r")
while (length(next.line <- readLines(conn, n=1)) > 0) {
 split.line <- strsplit(next.line, "\t")
 key <- split.line[[1]][1]
 val <- as.numeric(split.line[[1]][2])
 if (is.na(current.key)) {
 current.key <- key
 current.val <- val
 }
 else {
 if (current.key == key) {
current.val <- current.val + val
}
else {
write(paste(current.key, current.val, sep="\t"), stdout())
current.key <- key
current.val<- val
}
}
}
write(paste(current.key, current.val, sep="\t"), stdout())
close(conn)
```

From the following codes, we run MapReduce in R without installing or using any R library/package. There is one `system()` method in R to fire the system command within R console to help us direct the firing of Hadoop jobs within R. It will also provide the repose of the commands into the R console.

```
# For locating at Hadoop Directory
system("cd $HADOOP_HOME")


# For listing all HDFS first level directory
system("bin/hadoop dfs -ls /")


# For running Hadoop MapReduce with streaming parameters
system(paste("bin/hadoop jar
/usr/local/hadoop/contrib/streaming/hadoop-streaming-1.0.3.jar ",

" -input /stock/table.csv",
" -output /stock/outputs",
" -file /usr/local/hadoop/stock/stock_mapper.R",
" -mapper /usr/local/hadoop/stock/stock_mapper.R",
" -file /usr/local/hadoop/stock/stock_reducer.R",
" -reducer /usr/local/hadoop/stock/stock_reducer.R"))


# For storing the output of list command
dir <- system("bin/hadoop dfs -ls /stock/outputs", intern=TRUE)
dir


# For storing the output from part-oooo (output file)
out <- system("bin/hadoop dfs -cat /stock/outputs/part-00000",
intern=TRUE)


# displaying Hadoop MapReduce output data out
```

You can also run this same program via the terminal:

```
bin/hadoop jar /usr/local/hadoop/contrib/streaming/hadoop-streaming-
1.0.3.jar \

 -input /stock/table.csv \
 -output /stock/outputs\
 -file /usr/local/hadoop/stock/stock_mapper.R \
 -mapper /usr/local/hadoop/stock/stock_mapper.R \
 -file /usr/local/hadoop/stock/stock_reducer.R \
 -reducer /usr/local/hadoop/stock/stock_reducer.R
```

While running this program, the output at your R console or terminal will be as given in the following screenshot, and with the help of this we can monitor the status of the Hadoop MapReduce job. Here we will see them sequentially with the divided parts. Please note that we have separated the logs output into parts to help you understand them better.

The MapReduce log output contains (when run from terminal):

- With this initial portion of log, we can identify the metadata for the Hadoop MapReduce job. We can also track the job status with the web browser, by calling the given `Tracking URL`. This is how the MapReduce job metadata is tracked.

```
packageJobJar: [/usr/local/hadoop/cma/stock_mapper.R, /usr/local/hadoop/cma/stock_reducer.R,
/app/hadoop/tmp/hadoop-unjar6788909629320597592/] [] /tmp/streamjob5343401846101499553.jar tmpDir=null
13/08/25 09:40:21 INFO util.NativeCodeLoader: Loaded the native-hadoop library
13/08/25 09:40:21 WARN snappy.LoadSnappy: Snappy native library not loaded
13/08/25 09:40:21 INFO mapred.FileInputFormat: Total input paths to process : 1
13/08/25 09:40:22 INFO streaming.StreamJob: getLocalDirs(): [/app/hadoop/tmp/mapred/local]
13/08/25 09:40:22 INFO streaming.StreamJob: Running job: job_201308250742_0009
13/08/25 09:40:22 INFO streaming.StreamJob: To kill this job, run:
13/08/25 09:40:22 INFO streaming.StreamJob: /usr/local/hadoop/libexec/../bin/hadoop job  -Dmapred.job.tracker=localhost:54311
 -kill job_201308250742_0009
13/08/25 09:40:22 INFO streaming.StreamJob: Tracking URL: http://localhost:50030/jobdetails.jsp?jobid=job_201308250742_0009
```

- With this portion of log, we can monitor the status of the Mapper or Reducer tasks being run on the Hadoop cluster to get the details like whether it was successful or failed. This is how we track the status of the Mapper and Reducer tasks.

```
13/08/0:23 INFO streaming.StreamJob:
map 0%   reduce 0%

13/08/25 09:41:39 INFO streaming.StreamJob:
map 29%  reduce 0%

13/08/25 09:41:43 INFO streaming.StreamJob:
map 59%  reduce 0%

13/08/25 09:41:58 INFO streaming.StreamJob:
map 79%  reduce 0%

13/08/25 09:42:01 INFO streaming.StreamJob:
map 100%  reduce 0%

13/08/25 09:42:44 INFO streaming.StreamJob:
map 100%  reduce 100%

13/08/25 09:43:02 INFO streaming.StreamJob:
Job complete: job_201308250742_0009
```

- Once the MapReduce job is completed, its output location will be displayed at the end of the logs. This is known as tracking the HDFS output location.

```
13/08/25 09:43:02 INFO streaming.StreamJob:
Output: /stock/outputs
```

- From the terminal, the output of the Hadoop MapReduce program can be called using the following command:

```
bin/hadoop dfs -cat /stock/outputs/part-00000
```

- The headers of the output of your MapReduce program will look as follows:

`change    frequency`

- The following figure shows the sample output of MapReduce problem:

```
-0.00999999999999091    2
-0.00999999999999801     13
-0.0100000000000051    7
-0.019999999999996     11
-0.0200000000000031      19
-0.029999999999994    2
-0.0300000000000011      23
-0.039999999999992     2
-0.039999999999991       15
-0.0400000000000063      6
-0.049999999999972       27
-0.0500000000000043      8
-0.0599999999999952      9
-0.0600000000000023      34
-0.069999999999932       5
-0.0700000000000003      21
-0.0700000000000074      2
-0.0799999999999983      20
-0.0800000000000054      5
   4.12      2
   4.19      1
   4.25      1
   4.37      1
   4.5      1
   4.88      1
   5      1
   5.19      1
   5.38      1
   7.69      1
```

Visualizing data

We can get more insights if we visualize our output with various graphs in R. Here, we have tried to visualize the output with the help of the `ggplot2` package.

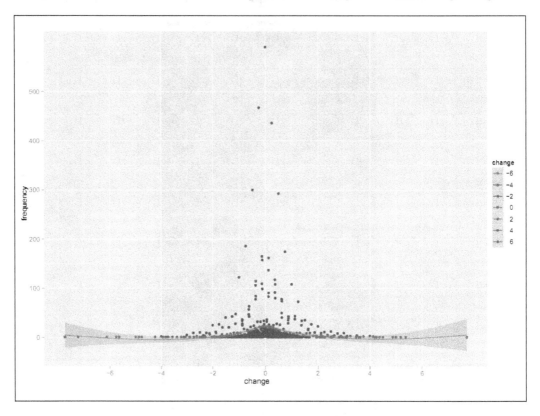

From the previous graph, we can quickly identify that most of the time the stock price has changed from around 0 to 1.5. So, the stock's price movements in the history will be helpful at the time of investing.

The required code for generating this graph is as follows:

```
# Loading ggplot2 library
library(ggplot2);

# we have stored above terminal output to stock_output.txt file

#loading it to R workspace
myStockData <- read.delim("stock_output.txt", header=F, sep="",
dec=".");

# plotting the data with ggplot2 geom_smooth function
ggplot(myStockData, aes(x=V1, y=V2)) + geom_smooth() + geom_point();
```

In the next section, we have included the case study on how Big Data analytics is performed with R and Hadoop for the **Kaggle** data competition.

Predicting the sale price of blue book for bulldozers – case study

This is a case study for predicting the auction sale price for a piece of heavy equipment to create a blue book for bulldozers.

Identifying the problem

In this example, I have included a case study by Cloudera data scientists on how large datasets can be resampled, and applied the random forest model with R and Hadoop. Here, I have considered the Kaggle blue book for bulldozers competition for understanding the types of Big Data problem definitions. Here, the goal of this competition is to predict the sale price of a particular piece of heavy equipment at a usage auction based on its usage, equipment type, and configuration. This solution has been provided by *Uri Laserson* (Data Scientist at Cloudera). The provided data contains the information about auction result posting, usage, and equipment configuration.

It's a trick to model the Big Data sets and divide them into the smaller datasets. Fitting the model on that dataset is a traditional machine learning technique such as random forests or bagging. There are possibly two reasons for random forests:

- Large datasets typically live in a cluster, so any operations will have some level of parallelism. Separate models fit on separate nodes that contain different subsets of the initial data.

- Even if you can use the entire initial dataset to fit a single model, it turns out that ensemble methods, where you fit multiple smaller models by using subsets of data, generally outperform single models. Indeed, fitting a single model with 100M data points can perform worse than fitting just a few models with 10M data points each (so smaller total data outperforms larger total data).

Sampling with replacement is the most popular method for sampling from the initial dataset for producing a collection of samples for model fitting. This method is equivalent to sampling from a multinomial distribution, where the probability of selecting any individual input data point is uniform over the entire dataset.

 Kaggle is a Big Data platform where data scientists from all over the world compete to solve Big Data analytics problems hosted by data-driven organizations.

Designing data requirement

For this competition, Kaggle has provided real-world datasets that comprises approximately 4,00,000 training data points. Each data point represents the various attributes of sales, configuration of the bulldozer, and sale price. To find out where to predict the sales price, the random forest regression model needs to be implemented.

> The reference link for this Kaggle competition is http://www.kaggle.com/c/bluebook-for-bulldozers. You can check the data, information, forum, and leaderboard as well as explore some other Big Data analytics competitions and participate in them to evaluate your data analytics skills.

We chose this model because we are interested in predicting the sales price in numeric values from random sets of a large dataset.

The datasets are provided in the terms of the following data files:

File name	Description format (size)
Train	This is a training set that contains data for 2011.
Valid	This is a validation set that contains data from January 1, 2012 to April 30, 2012.
Data dictionary	This is the metadata of the training dataset variables.
Machine_Appendix	This contains the correct year of manufacturing for a given machine along with the make, model, and product class details.
Test	This tests datasets.
random_forest_benchmark_test	This is the benchmark solution provided by the host.

> In case you want to learn and practice Big Data analytics, you can acquire the Big Data sets from the Kaggle data source by participating in the Kaggle data competitions. These contain the datasets of various fields from industries worldwide.

Preprocessing data

To perform the analytics over the provided Kaggle datasets, we need to build a predictive model. To predict the sale price for the auction, we will fit the model over provided datasets. But the datasets are provided with more than one file. So we will merge them as well as perform data augmentation for acquiring more meaningful data. We are going to build a model from `Train.csv` and `Machine_Appendix.csv` for better prediction of the sale price.

Here are the data preprocessing tasks that need to be performed over the datasets:

```
# Loading Train.csv dataset which includes the Sales as well as
machine identifier data attributes.

transactions <- read.table(file="~/Downloads/Train.csv",
header=TRUE,
sep=",",
quote="\"",
row.names=1,
fill=TRUE,
colClasses=c(MachineID="factor",
 ModelID="factor",
datasource="factor",
YearMade="character",
SalesID="character",
auctioneerID="factor",
UsageBand="factor",
saledate="custom.date.2",
Tire_Size="tire.size",
Undercarriage_Pad_Width="undercarriage",
Stick_Length="stick.length"),
na.strings=na.values)


# Loading Machine_Appendix.csv for machine configuration information

machines <- read.table(file="~/Downloads/Machine_Appendix.csv",
header=TRUE,
sep=",",
quote="\"",
fill=TRUE,
colClasses=c(MachineID="character",
ModelID="factor",
fiManufacturerID="factor"),
na.strings=na.values)
```

```
# Updating the values to numeric
# updating sale data number
transactions$saledatenumeric <- as.numeric(transactions$saledate)
transactions$ageAtSale <- as.numeric(transactions$saledate -
as.Date(transactions$YearMade, format="%Y"))

transactions$saleYear <- as.numeric(format(transactions$saledate,
"%Y"))

# updating the month of sale from transaction
transactions$saleMonth <- as.factor(format(transactions$saledate,
"%B"))

# updating the date of sale from transaction
transactions$saleDay <- as.factor(format(transactions$saledate, "%d"))

# updating the day of week of sale from transaction
transactions$saleWeekday <- as.factor(format(transactions$saledate,
"%A"))

# updating the year of sale from transaction
transactions$YearMade <- as.integer(transactions$YearMade)

# deriving the model price from transaction
transactions$MedianModelPrice <- unsplit(lapply(split(transactions$Sa
lePrice,
transactions$ModelID), median), transactions$ModelID)


# deriving the model count from transaction
transactions$ModelCount <- unsplit(lapply(split(transactions$SalePri
ce, transactions$ModelID), length), transactions$ModelID)

# Merging the transaction and machine data in to dataframe
training.data <- merge(x=transactions, y=machines, by="MachineID")

# write denormalized data out
write.table(x=training.data,
file="~/temp/training.csv",
sep=",",
quote=TRUE,
row.names=FALSE,
eol="\n",
col.names=FALSE)
# Create poisson directory at HDFS
bin/hadoop dfs -mkdir /poisson

# Uploading file training.csv at HDFS
bin/hadoop dfs -put ~/temp/training.csv /poisson/
```

Performing analytics over data

As we are going to perform analytics with sampled datasets, we need to understand how many datasets need to be sampled.

For random sampling, we have considered three model parameters, which are as follows:

- We have N data points in our initial training set. This is very large (10^6-10^9) and is distributed over an HDFS cluster.

- We are going to train a set of M different models for an ensemble classifier.

- Each of the M models will be fitted with K data points, where typically K << N. (For example, K may be 1-10 percent of N.).

We have N numbers of training datasets, which are fixed and generally outside our control. As we are going to handle this via **Poisson** sampling, we need to define the total number of input vectors to be consumed into the random forest model.

There are three cases to be considered:

- **KM < N**: In this case, we are not using the full amount of data available to us

- **KM = N**: In this case, we can exactly partition our dataset to produce totally independent samples

- **KM > N**: In this case, we must resample some of our data with replacements

The Poisson sampling method described in the following section handles all the three cases in the same framework. However, note that for the case KM = N, it does not partition the data, but simply resamples it.

Understanding Poisson-approximation resampling

Generalized linear models are an extension of the general linear model. Poisson regression is a situation of generalized models. The dependent variable obeys Poisson distribution.

Poisson sampling will be run on the Map of the MapReduce task because it occurs for input data points. This doesn't guarantee that every data point will be considered into the model, which is better than multinomial resampling of full datasets. But it will guarantee the generation of independent samples by using N training input points.

Here, the following graph indicates the amount of missed datasets that can be retrieved in the Poisson sampling with the function of KM/N:

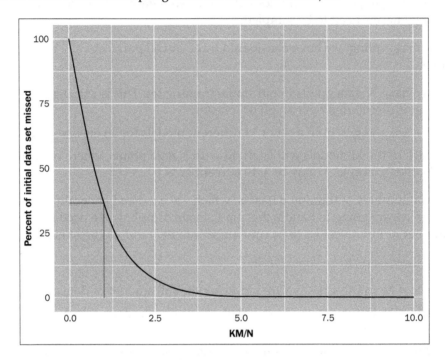

The grey line indicates the value of KM=N. Now, let's look at the pseudo code of the MapReduce algorithm. We have used three parameters: N, M, and K where K is fixed. We used T=K/N to eliminate the need for the value of N in advance.

- **An example of sampling parameters**: Here, we will implement the preceding logic with a pseudo code. We will start by defining two model input parameters as `frac.per.model` and `num.models`, where `frac.per.model` is used for defining the fraction of the full dataset that can be used, and `num.models` is used for defining how many models will be fitted from the dataset.

  ```
  T = 0.1  # param 1: K / N-average fraction of input data in each
  model 10%
  
  M = 50   # param 2: number of models
  ```

- **Logic of Mapper**: Mapper will be designed for generating the samples of the full dataset by data wrangling.

```
def map(k, v):
// for each input data point
    for i in 1:M
    // for each model
        m = Poisson(T)
    // num times curr point should appear in this sample
        if m > 0
            for j in 1:m
    // emit current input point proper num of times
                emit (i, v)
```

- **Logic of Reducer**: Reducer will take a data sample as input and fit the random forest model over it.

```
def reduce(k, v):
    fit model or calculate statistic with the sample in v
```

Fitting random forests with RHadoop

In machine learning, fitting a model means fitting the best line into our data. Fitting a model can fall under several types, namely, under fitting, over fitting, and normal fitting. In case of under and over fitting, there are chances of high bias (cross validation and training errors are high) and high variance (cross validation error is high but training error is low) effects, which is not good. We will normally fit the model over the datasets.

Here are the diagrams for fitting a model over datasets with three types of fitting:

- **Under fitting**: In this cross validation and training errors are high

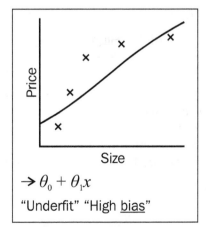

- **Normal fitting**: In this cross-validation and training errors are normal

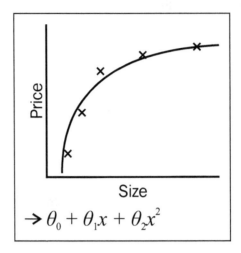

$$\rightarrow \theta_0 + \theta_1 x + \theta_2 x^2$$

- **Over fitting**: In this the cross-validation error is high but training error is low

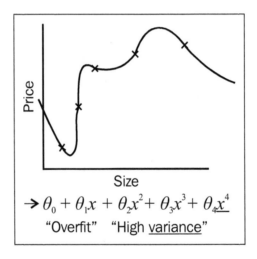

$$\rightarrow \theta_0 + \theta_1 x + \theta_2 x^2 + \theta_3 x^3 + \theta_4 x^4$$

"Overfit" "High variance"

We will fit the model over the data using the random forest technique of machine learning. This is a type of recursive partitioning method, particularly well suited for small and large problems. It involves an ensemble (or set) of classification (or regression) trees that are calculated on random subsets of the data, using a subset of randomly restricted and selected predictors for every split in each classification tree.

Furthermore, the results of an ensemble of classification/regression trees have been used to produce better predictions instead of using the results of just one classification tree.

We will now implement our Poisson sampling strategy with RHadoop. We will start by setting global values for our parameters:

```
#10% of input data to each sample on avg
frac.per.model <- 0.1
num.models <- 50
```

Let's check how to implement Mapper as per the specifications in the pseudo code with RHadoop.

- Mapper is implemented in the the following manner:

```
poisson.subsample <- function(k, input) {
  # this function is used to generate a sample from the current
block of data
  generate.sample <- function(i) {
    # generate N Poisson variables
    draws <- rpois(n=nrow(input), lambda=frac.per.model)
    # compute the index vector for the corresponding rows,
    # weighted by the number of Poisson draws
    indices <- rep((1:nrow(input)), draws)
    # emit the rows; RHadoop takes care of replicating the key
appropriately
    # and rbinding the data frames from different mappers together
for the
    # reducer
    keyval(i, input[indices, ])
  }

  # here is where we generate the actual sampled data
  c.keyval(lapply(1:num.models, generate.sample))
}
```

Since we are using R, it's tricky to fit the model with the random forest model over the collected sample dataset.

- Reducer is implemented in the following manner:

```
# REDUCE function
fit.trees <- function(k, v) {
  # rmr rbinds the emitted values, so v is a dataframe
  # note that do.trace=T is used to produce output to stderr to keep
the reduce task from timing out
  rf <- randomForest(formula=model.formula,
                     data=v,
                     na.action=na.roughfix,
                     ntree=10,
                     do.trace=FALSE)

 # rf is a list so wrap it in another list to ensure that only
 # one object gets emitted. this is because keyval is vectorized
  keyval(k, list(forest=rf))
}
```

- To fit the model, we need `model.formula`, which is as follows:

```
model.formula <- SalePrice ~ datasource + auctioneerID + YearMade
+ saledatenumeric + ProductSize + ProductGroupDesc.x + Enclosure
+ Hydraulics + ageAtSale + saleYear + saleMonth + saleDay +
saleWeekday + MedianModelPrice + ModelCount + MfgYear
```

`SalePrice` is defined as a response variable and the rest of them are defined as predictor variables for the random forest model.

 Random forest model with R doesn't support factor with level more than 32.

- The MapReduce job can be executed using the following command:

```
mapreduce(input="/poisson/training.csv",
          input.format=bulldozer.input.format,
          map=poisson.subsample,
          reduce=fit.trees,
          output="/poisson/output")
```

The resulting trees are dumped in HDFS at /poisson/output.

- Finally, we can load the trees, merge them, and use them to classify new test points:

```
mraw.forests <- values(from.dfs("/poisson/output"))
forest <- do.call(combine, raw.forests)
```

Each of the 50 samples produced a random forest with 10 trees, so the final random forest is a collection of 500 trees, fitted in a distributed fashion over a Hadoop cluster.

> The full set of source files is available on the official Cloudera blog at `http://blog.cloudera.com/blog/2013/02/how-to-resample-from-a-large-data-set-in-parallel-with-r-on-hadoop/`.

Hopefully, we have learned a scalable approach for training ensemble classifiers or bootstrapping in a parallel fashion by using a Poisson approximation for multinomial sampling.

Summary

In this chapter, we learned how to perform Big Data analytics with various data driven activities over an R and Hadoop integrated environment.

In the next chapter, we will learn more about how R and Hadoop can be used to perform machine learning techniques.

6
Understanding Big Data Analysis with Machine Learning

In this chapter, we are going to learn about different machine learning techniques that can be used with R and Hadoop to perform Big Data analytics with the help of the following points:

- Introduction to machine learning
- Types of machine-learning algorithms
- Supervised machine-learning algorithms
- Unsupervised machine-learning algorithms
- Recommendation algorithms

Introduction to machine learning

Machine learning is a branch of artificial intelligence that allows us to make our application intelligent without being explicitly programmed. Machine learning concepts are used to enable applications to take a decision from the available datasets. A combination of machine learning and data mining can be used to develop spam mail detectors, self-driven cars, speech recognition, face recognition, and online transactional fraud-activity detection.

There are many popular organizations that are using machine-learning algorithms to make their service or product understand the need of their users and provide services as per their behavior. Google has its intelligent web search engine, which provides a number one search, spam classification in Google Mail, news labeling in Google News, and Amazon for recommender systems. There are many open source frameworks available for developing these types of applications/frameworks, such as R, Python, Apache Mahout, and Weka.

Types of machine-learning algorithms

There are three different types of machine-learning algorithms for intelligent system development:

- Supervised machine-learning algorithms
- Unsupervised machine-learning algorithms
- Recommender systems

In this chapter, we are going to discuss well-known business problems with classification, regression, and clustering, as well as how to perform these machine-learning techniques over Hadoop to overcome memory issues.

If you load a dataset that won't be able to fit into your machine memories and you try to run it, the predictive analysis will throw an error related to machine memory, such as **Error: cannot allocate vector of size 990.1 MB**. The solution is to increase the machine configuration or parallelize with commodity hardware.

Supervised machine-learning algorithms

In this section, we will be learning about supervised machine-learning algorithms. The algorithms are as follows:

- Linear regression
- Logistic regression

Linear regression

Linear regression is mainly used for predicting and forecasting values based on historical information. Regression is a supervised machine-learning technique to identify the linear relationship between target variables and explanatory variables. We can say it is used for predicting the target variable values in numeric form.

In the following section, we will be learning about linear regression with R and linear regression with R and Hadoop.

Here, the variables that are going to be predicted are considered as target variables and the variables that are going to help predict the target variables are called explanatory variables. With the linear relationship, we can identify the impact of a change in explanatory variables on the target variable.

In mathematics, regression can be formulated as follows:

$$y = ax + e$$

Other formulae include:

- The slope of the regression line is given by:

$$a = (N\Sigma xy - (\Sigma x)(\Sigma y)) / (N\Sigma x^2 - (\Sigma x)^2)$$

- The intercept point of regression is given by:

$$e = (\Sigma y - b(\Sigma x)) / N$$

Here, x and y are variables that form a dataset and N is the total numbers of values.

Suppose we have the data shown in the following table:

x	y
63	3.1
64	3.6
65	3.8
66	4

If we have a new value of x, we can get the value of y with it with the help of the regression formula.

Applications of linear regression include:

- Sales forecasting
- Predicting optimum product price
- Predicting the next online purchase from various sources and campaigns

Let's look at the statistical technique to implement the regression model for the provided dataset. Assume that we have been given n number of statistical data units.

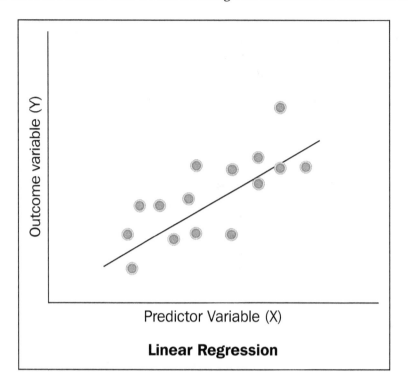

Its formula is as follows:

$$Y = e_0 + a_0x_0 + a_1x_1 + a_2x_2 + a_3x_3 + a_4x_4$$

Here, Y is the target variable (response variable), xi are explanatory variables, and e_0 is the sum of the squared error term, which can be considered as noise. To get a more accurate prediction, we need to reduce this error term as soon as possible with the help of the `call` function.

Linear regression with R

Now we will see how to perform linear regression in R. We can use the in-built `lm()` method to build a linear regression model with R.

```
Model <-lm(target ~ ex_var1, data=train_dataset)
```

It will build a regression model based on the property of the provided dataset and store all of the variables' coefficients and model parameters used for predicting and identifying of data pattern from the model variable values.

```
# Defining data variables
X = matrix(rnorm(2000), ncol = 10)
y = as.matrix(rnorm(200))

# Bundling data variables into dataframe
train_data <- data.frame(X,y)

# Training model for generating prediction
lmodel<- lm(y~ train_data $X1 + train_data $X2 + train_data $X3 +
train_data $X4 + train_data $X5 + train_data $X6 + train_data $X7 +
train_data $X8 + train_data $X9 + train_data $X10,data= train_data)

summary(lmodel)
```

The following are the various model parameters that can be displayed with the preceding summary command:

- **RSS**: This is equal to $\sum$(yactual - y)^2.

- **Degrees of Freedom (DOF)**: This is used for identifying the degree of fit for the prediction model, which should be as small as possible (logically, the value 0 means perfect prediction).

- **Residual standard error (RSS/DF)**: This is used for identifying the goodness of fit for the prediction model, which should be as small as possible (logically, the value 0 means perfect prediction).

- **pr**: This is the probability for a variable to be included into the model; it should be less than 0.05 for a variable to be included.

- **t-value**: This is equal to 15.

- **f**: This is the statistic that checks whether R square is a value other than zero.

```
> summary(lmodel)

Call:
lm(formula = y ~ train_data$X1 + train_data$X2 + train_data$X3 +
    train_data$X4 + train_data$X5 + train_data$X6 + train_data$X7 +
    train_data$X8 + train_data$X9 + train_data$X10, data = train_data)

Residuals:
     Min       1Q   Median       3Q      Max
-2.63032 -0.63309 -0.07399  0.62334  2.83372

Coefficients:
                Estimate Std. Error t value Pr(>|t|)
(Intercept)    -0.166414   0.070605  -2.357  0.01945 *
train_data$X1   0.031970   0.071050   0.450  0.65325
train_data$X2  -0.089957   0.072481  -1.241  0.21611
train_data$X3   0.067545   0.069906   0.966  0.33517
train_data$X4   0.187189   0.071434   2.620  0.00949 **
train_data$X5  -0.049948   0.072221  -0.692  0.49004
train_data$X6   0.019923   0.071427   0.279  0.78060
train_data$X7   0.013168   0.074747   0.176  0.86035
train_data$X8   0.079554   0.074907   1.062  0.28957
train_data$X9  -0.008961   0.068948  -0.130  0.89674
train_data$X10 -0.110755   0.067407  -1.643  0.10203
---
Signif. codes:  0 '***' 0.001 '**' 0.01 '*' 0.05 '.' 0.1 ' ' 1

Residual standard error: 0.9841 on 189 degrees of freedom
Multiple R-squared:  0.06692,  Adjusted R-squared:  0.01755
F-statistic: 1.355 on 10 and 189 DF,  p-value: 0.204
```

Linear regression with R and Hadoop

Assume we have a large dataset. How will we perform regression data analysis now? In such cases, we can use R and Hadoop integration to perform parallel linear regression by implementing Mapper and Reducer. It will divide the dataset into chunks among the available nodes and then they will process the distributed data in parallel. It will not fire memory issues when we run with an R and Hadoop cluster because the large dataset is going to be distributed and processed with R among Hadoop computation nodes. Also, keep in mind that this implemented method does not provide higher prediction accuracy than the lm() model.

RHadoop is used here for integration of R and Hadoop, which is a trusted open source distribution of **Revolution Analytics**. For more information on RHadoop, visit https://github.com/RevolutionAnalytics/RHadoop/wiki. Among the packages of RHadoop, here we are using only the rmr and rhdfs libraries.

Let's see how to perform regression analysis with R and Hadoop data technologies.

```
# Defining the datasets with Big Data matrix X
X = matrix(rnorm(20000), ncol = 10)
X.index = to.dfs(cbind(1:nrow(X), X))
y = as.matrix(rnorm(2000))
```

Here, the Sum() function is re-usable as shown in the following code:

```
# Function defined to be used as reducers
Sum =
  function(., YY)
    keyval(1, list(Reduce('+', YY)))
```

The outline of the linear regression algorithm is as follows:

1. Calculating the Xtx value with MapReduce job1.
2. Calculating the Xty value with MapReduce job2.
3. Deriving the coefficient values with Solve (Xtx, Xty).

Let's understand these steps one by one.

The first step is to calculate the `Xtx` value with MapReduce job 1.

1. The big matrix is passed to the Mapper in chunks of complete rows. Smaller cross-products are computed for these submatrices and passed on to a single Reducer, which sums them together. Since we have a single key, a Combiner is mandatory and since the matrix sum is associative and commutative, we certainly can use it here.

```
# XtX =
  values(

# For loading hdfs data in to R
    from.dfs(

# MapReduce Job to produce XT*X
      mapreduce(
        input = X.index,

# Mapper - To calculate and emitting XT*X
        map =
          function(., Xi) {
            yi = y[Xi[,1],]
            Xi = Xi[,-1]
            keyval(1, list(t(Xi) %*% Xi))},

# Reducer - To reduce the Mapper output by performing sum
operation over them
        reduce = Sum,
        combine = TRUE)))[[1]]
```

2. When we have a large amount of data stored in **Hadoop Distributed File System (HDFS)**, we need to pass its path value to the input parameters in the `MapReduce` method.

3. In the preceding code, we saw that x is the design matrix, which has been created with the following function:

```
X = matrix(rnorm(2000), ncol = 10)
```

4. Its output will look as shown in the following screenshot:

```
> x = matrix(rnorm(2000), ncol = 10)
> x
            [,1]         [,2]         [,3]         [,4]        [,5]        [,6]        [,7]        [,8]        [,9]       [,10]
 [1,] -1.331009728 -0.938595642  0.251500253 -0.38732670  1.726157283  1.28011442 -1.188795165  0.65626505 -0.13358852  1.994043068
 [2,]  0.565496539  1.736337940 -1.073862937  1.50055477 -0.804540417 -1.00173291 -0.071578111  0.74791167 -3.20628276 -0.195105803
 [3,]  0.850172588 -1.392844682 -0.471156772 -0.55026420  0.517891403 -1.12981861 -0.322102941 -0.16226288 -0.08717879  1.107455933
 [4,]  0.444142274 -1.820468066 -0.969811221  0.57173997  0.557294449  0.43355504 -0.437071473 -0.86645597 -0.58256758 -1.718820466
 [5,]  0.507975469  0.506769942  0.252459216  0.95632941 -0.029616669 -0.04784847 -2.051021993 -0.42139955 -1.32394457  0.065074504
 [6,]  0.555452856  1.177174158 -0.622080442 -0.75767182  0.755015836 -0.84369878  0.832374670  0.54215290  0.13627573  0.794320048
 [7,]  0.380677838  0.293751554 -2.026362457 -0.11989566 -1.169743342  3.79201075 -0.987848608 -0.60910066  0.07366394 -0.810556332
 [8,] -2.468886553 -1.346583151 -0.526052331  0.28194997  1.373465723  0.65055228 -2.472305833 -1.43318203  0.75182640 -0.636107506
 [9,] -1.342776078  0.776121876 -0.426102128 -0.39707018 -1.506004183 -0.32216979 -1.087819697  0.03844442  0.31546613  0.697446509
[10,] -0.991048535  0.528419049 -2.483191832  0.08032207 -3.034221103  0.59355980  1.389037960 -1.52551162 -0.71786713  2.175064443
[11,] -0.783163703  0.350780313  0.122302766  0.54048200  0.615773536 -1.51988600 -0.012335649 -0.30434678  0.77427398  0.374912625
[12,]  0.634190858  0.351298779  0.462613539  0.32182266  0.527092302  1.29092352  0.195931327  1.18545674 -0.59230294  0.156119417
```

So, here all the columns will be considered as explanatory variables and their standard errors can be calculated in a similar manner to how we calculated them with normal linear regression.

To calculate the `Xty` value with MapReduce job 2 is pretty much the same as for the vector `y`, which is available to the nodes according to normal scope rules.

```
Xty = values(

# For loading hdfs data
from.dfs(

# MapReduce job to produce XT * y
        mapreduce(
            input = X.index,

# Mapper - To calculate and emitting XT*y
            map = function(., Xi) {
                yi = y[Xi[,1],]
                Xi = Xi[,-1]
                keyval(1, list(t(Xi) %*% yi))},

# Reducer - To reducer the Mapper output by performing # sum
operation over them
                reduce = Sum,
                combine = TRUE)))[[1]]
```

To derive the coefficient values with `solve (Xtx, Xty)`, use the following steps:

1. Finally, we just need to call the following line of code to get the coefficient values.

```
solve(XtX, Xty)
```

2. The output of the preceding command will be as shown in the following screenshot:

```
> solve(XtX, Xty)
            [,1]
 [1,]  0.038845121
 [2,]  0.015100617
 [3,]  0.012841903
 [4,] -0.033987022
 [5,] -0.004162355
 [6,] -0.175773152
 [7,] -0.080512728
 [8,]  0.036393052
 [9,] -0.063170450
[10,]  0.073065252
```

Logistic regression

In statistics, logistic regression or logit regression is a type of probabilistic classification model. Logistic regression is used extensively in numerous disciplines, including the medical and social science fields. It can be binomial or multinomial.

Binary logistic regression deals with situations in which the outcome for a dependent variable can have two possible types. Multinomial logistic regression deals with situations where the outcome can have three or more possible types.

Logistic regression can be implemented using logistic functions, which are listed here.

- To predict the log odds ratios, use the following formula:

  $logit(p) = \beta 0 + \beta 1 \times x1 + \beta 2 \times x2 + ... + \beta n \times xn$

- The probability formula is as follows:

  $p = e^{logit(p)} / 1 + e^{logit(p)}$

logit(p) is a linear function of the explanatory variable, X (x1,x2,x3..xn), which is similar to linear regression. So, the output of this function will be in the range 0 to 1. Based on the probability score, we can set its probability range from 0 to 1. In a majority of the cases, if the score is greater than 0.5, it will be considered as 1, otherwise 0. Also, we can say it provides a classification boundary to classify the outcome variable.

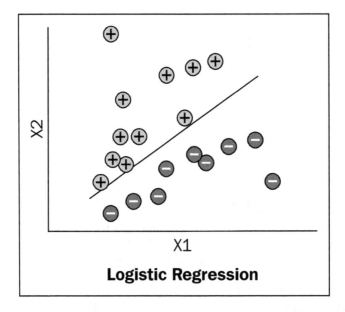

The preceding figure is of a training dataset. Based on the training dataset plot, we can say there is one classification boundary generated by the glm model in R.

Applications of logistic regression include:

- Predicting the likelihood of an online purchase
- Detecting the presence of diabetes

25

Logistic regression with R

To perform logistic regression with R, we will use the `iris` dataset and the `glm` model.

```
#loading iris dataset
data(iris)

# Setting up target variable
target <- data.frame(isSetosa=(iris$Species == 'setosa'))

# Adding target to iris and creating new dataset
inputdata <- cbind(target,iris)

# Defining the logistic regression formula
formula <- isSetosa ~ Sepal.Length + Sepal.Width + Petal.Length +
Petal.Width

# running Logistic model via glm()
logisticModel <- glm(formula, data=inputdata, family="binomial")
```

Logistic regression with R and Hadoop

To perform logistic regression with R and Hadoop, we will use RHadoop with `rmr2`.

The outline of the logistic regression algorithm is as follows:

- Defining the `lr.map` Mapper function
- Defining the `lr.reducer` Reducer function
- Defining the `logistic.regression` MapReduce function

Let's understand them one by one.

We will first define the logistic regression function with gradient decent. Multivariate regression can be performed by forming the nondependent variable into a matrix data format. For factorial variables, we can translate them to binary variables for fitting the model. This function will ask for `input`, `iterations`, `dims`, and `alpha` as input parameters.

- `lr.map`: This stands for the logistic regression Mapper, which will compute the contribution of subset points to the gradient.

```
# Mapper - computes the contribution of a subset of points to the
gradient.

lr.map =
    function(., M) {
        Y = M[,1]
        X = M[,-1]
        keyval(
          1,
          Y * X *
            g(-Y * as.numeric(X %*% t(plane)))))}
```

- `lr.reducer`: This stands for the logistic regression Reducer, which is performing just a big sum of all the values of key 1.

```
# Reducer - Perform sum operation over Mapper output.

lr.reduce =
    function(k, Z)
        keyval(k, t(as.matrix(apply(Z,2,sum))))
```

- `logistic.regression`: This will mainly define the `logistic.regression` MapReduce function with the following input parameters. Calling this function will start executing logistic regression of the MapReduce function.

    - `input`: This is an input dataset
    - `iterations`: This is the fixed number of iterations for calculating the gradient
    - `dims`: This is the dimension of input variables
    - `alpha`: This is the learning rate

Let's see how to develop the logistic regression function.

```
# MapReduce job - Defining MapReduce function for executing logistic
regression

logistic.regression =
  function(input, iterations, dims, alpha){
  plane = t(rep(0, dims))
  g = function(z) 1/(1 + exp(-z))
  for (i in 1:iterations) {
    gradient =
      values(
        from.dfs(
          mapreduce(
            input,
            map = lr.map,
            reduce = lr.reduce,
            combine = T)))
    plane = plane + alpha * gradient }
  plane }
```

Let's run this logistic regression function as follows:

```
# Loading dataset
data(foodstamp)

# Storing data to hdfs
testdata <-  to.dfs(as.matrix(foodstamp))

# Running logistic regression with R and Hadoop
print(logistic.regression(testdata,10,3,0.05))
```

The output of the preceding command will be as follows:

```
          TEN SUP    INC
[1,] 0.15 0.3 222.2
```

Unsupervised machine learning algorithm

In machine learning, unsupervised learning is used for finding the hidden structure from the unlabeled dataset. Since the datasets are not labeled, there will be no error while evaluating for potential solutions.

Unsupervised machine learning includes several algorithms, some of which are as follows:

- Clustering
- Artificial neural networks
- Vector quantization

We will consider popular clustering algorithms here.

Clustering

Clustering is the task of grouping a set of object in such a way that similar objects with similar characteristics are grouped in the same category, but other objects are grouped in other categories. In clustering, the input datasets are not labeled; they need to be labeled based on the similarity of their data structure.

In unsupervised machine learning, the classification technique performs the same procedure to map the data to a category with the help of the provided set of input training datasets. The corresponding procedure is known as clustering (or cluster analysis), and involves grouping data into categories based on some measure of inherent similarity; for example, the distance between data points.

From the following figure, we can identify clustering as grouping objects based on their similarity:

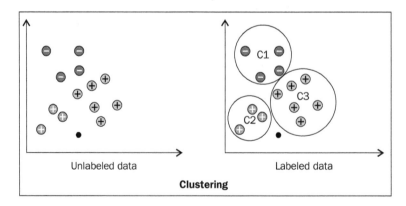

Clustering

There are several clustering techniques available within R libraries, such as k-means, k-medoids, hierarchical, and density-based clustering. Among them, k-means is widely used as the clustering algorithm in data science. This algorithm asks for a number of clusters to be the input parameters from the user side.

Applications of clustering are as follows:

- Market segmentation
- Social network analysis
- Organizing computer network
- Astronomical data analysis

Clustering with R

We are considering the `k-means` method here for implementing the clustering model over the `iris` input dataset, which can be achieved by just calling its in-built R dataset – the `iris` data (for more information, visit http://stat.ethz.ch/R-manual/R-devel/library/datasets/html/iris.html). Here we will see how k-means clustering can be performed with R.

```
# Loading iris flower dataset
data("iris")
# generating clusters for iris dataset
kmeans <- kmeans(iris[, -5], 3, iter.max = 1000)

# comparing iris Species with generated cluster points
Comp <- table(iris[, 5], kmeans$cluster)
```

Deriving clusters for small datasets is quite simple, but deriving it for huge datasets requires the use of Hadoop for providing computation power.

Performing clustering with R and Hadoop

Since the k-means clustering algorithm is already developed in RHadoop, we are going to use and understand it. You can make changes in their Mappers and Reducers as per the input dataset format. As we are dealing with Hadoop, we need to develop the Mappers and Reducers to be run on nodes in a parallel manner.

The outline of the clustering algorithm is as follows:

- Defining the `dist.fun` distance function
- Defining the `k-means.map` k-means Mapper function
- Defining the `k-means.reduce` k-means Reducer function
- Defining the `k-means.mr` k-means MapReduce function
- Defining input data points to be provided to the clustering algorithms

Now we will run `k-means.mr` (the k-means MapReduce job) by providing the required parameters.

Let's understand them one by one.

- `dist.fun`: First, we will see the `dist.fun` function for calculating the distance between a matrix of center C and a matrix of point P, which is tested. It can produce 10^6 points and 10^2 centers in five dimensions in approximately 16 seconds.

```
# distance calculation function
dist.fun =
      function(C, P) {
        apply(
          C,
          1,
          function(x)
            colSums((t(P) - x)^2))}
```

- `k-means.map`: The Mapper of the k-means MapReduce algorithm will compute the distance between points and all the centers and return the closest center for each point. This Mapper will run in iterations based on the following code. With the first iteration, the cluster center will be assigned randomly and from the next iteration, it will calculate these cluster centers based on the minimum distance from all the points of the cluster.

```
# k-Means Mapper
  kmeans.map =
      function(., P) {
        nearest = {

# First interations- Assign random cluster centers
        if(is.null(C))
          sample(
            1:num.clusters,
            nrow(P),
            replace = T)
```

```
# Rest of the iterations, where the clusters are assigned # based
on the minimum distance from points
        else {
            D = dist.fun(C, P)
            nearest = max.col(-D)}}

    if(!(combine || in.memory.combine))
        keyval(nearest, P)
    else
        keyval(nearest, cbind(1, P))}
```

- `k-means.reduce`: The Reducer of the k-means MapReduce algorithm will compute the column average of matrix points as key.

```
# k-Means Reducer
kmeans.reduce = {

# calculating the column average for both of the
# conditions

    if (!(combine || in.memory.combine) )
        function(., P)
            t(as.matrix(apply(P, 2, mean)))
    else
        function(k, P)
            keyval(
                k,
                t(as.matrix(apply(P, 2, sum)))))}
```

- `kmeans.mr`: Defining the k-means MapReduce function involves specifying several input parameters, which are as follows:
    - `P`: This denotes the input data points
    - `num.clusters`: This is the total number of clusters
    - `num.iter`: This is the total number of iterations to be processed with datasets
    - `combine`: This will decide whether the Combiner should be enabled or disabled (TRUE or FALSE)

```
# k-Means MapReduce - for
kmeans.mr =
    function(
        P,
```

```
            num.clusters,
            num.iter,
            combine,
            in.memory.combine) {
            C = NULL
            for(i in 1:num.iter ) {
              C =
                values(

# Loading hdfs dataset
                from.dfs(

# MapReduce job, with specification of input dataset,
# Mapper and Reducer
                  mapreduce(
                    P,
                    map = kmeans.map,
                    reduce = kmeans.reduce)))
            if(combine || in.memory.combine)
              C = C[, -1]/C[, 1]
            if(nrow(C) < num.clusters) {
              C =
                rbind(
                  C,
                  matrix(
                    rnorm(
                      (num.clusters -
                        nrow(C)) * nrow(C)),
                    ncol = nrow(C)) %*% C) }}
            C}
```

- Defining the input data points to be provided to the clustering algorithms:

```
# Input data points
P = do.call(
      rbind,
      rep(


        list(

# Generating Matrix of
          matrix(
# Generate random normalized data with sd = 10
            rnorm(10, sd = 10),
            ncol=2)),
        20)) +
      matrix(rnorm(200), ncol =2)
```

- Running `kmeans.mr` (the k-means MapReduce job) by providing it with the required parameters.

```
# Running kmeans.mr Hadoop MapReduce algorithms with providing the
required input parameters

kmeans.mr (
      to.dfs(P),
      num.clusters = 12,
      num.iter = 5,
      combine = FALSE,
      in.memory.combine = FALSE)
```

- The output of the preceding command is shown in the following screenshot:

```
              [,1]        [,2]
 [1,]   12.931487  -14.925114
 [2,]   12.513291    0.159962
 [3,]    3.997781   23.809110
 [4,]   13.235064   -2.456556
 [5,]   -3.331972   -9.848412
 [6,]   10.240459   56.584566
 [7,]   -3.364060   31.683668
 [8,]   19.370758   12.827422
 [9,]   -2.523515    7.471953
[10,]  -16.950461  -63.860343
[11,]    6.857692   18.418012
[12,]  -21.923976   35.914922
```

Recommendation algorithms

Recommendation is a machine-learning technique to predict what new items a user would like based on associations with the user's previous items. Recommendations are widely used in the field of e-commerce applications. Through this flexible data and behavior-driven algorithms, businesses can increase conversions by helping to ensure that relevant choices are automatically suggested to the right customers at the right time with cross-selling or up-selling.

For example, when a customer is looking for a Samsung Galaxy S IV/S4 mobile phone on Amazon, the store will also suggest other mobile phones similar to this one, presented in the **Customers Who Bought This Item Also Bought** window.

There are two different types of recommendations:

- **User-based recommendations**: In this type, users (customers) similar to current user (customer) are determined. Based on this user similarity, their interested/used items can be recommended to other users. Let's learn it through an example.

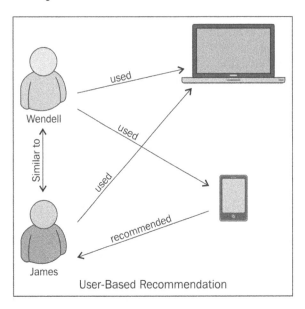

Assume there are two users named Wendell and James; both have a similar interest because both are using an iPhone. Wendell had used two items, iPad and iPhone, so James will be recommended to use iPad. This is user-based recommendation.

- **Item-based recommendations**: In this type, items similar to the items that are being currently used by a user are determined. Based on the item-similarity score, the similar items will be presented to the users for cross-selling and up-selling type of recommendations. Let's learn it through an example.

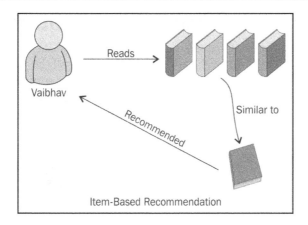

For example, a user named Vaibhav likes and uses the following books:

- *Apache Mahout Cookbook, Piero Giacomelli, Packt Publishing*
- *Hadoop MapReduce Cookbook, Thilina Gunarathne* and *Srinath Perera, Packt Publishing*
- *Hadoop Real-World Solutions Cookbook, Brian Femiano, Jon Lentz,* and *Jonathan R. Owens, Packt Publishing*
- *Big Data For Dummies, Dr. Fern Halper, Judith Hurwitz, Marcia Kaufman,* and *Alan Nugent, John Wiley & Sons Publishers*

Based on the preceding information, the recommender system will predict which new books Vaibhav would like to read, as follows:

- *Big Data Analytics with R and Hadoop, Vignesh Prajapati, Packt Publishing*

Now we will see how to generate recommendations with R and Hadoop. But before going towards the R and Hadoop combination, let us first see how to generate it with R. This will clear the concepts to translate your generated recommender systems to MapReduce recommendation algorithms. In case of generating recommendations with R and Hadoop, we will use the RHadoop distribution of **Revolution Analytics**.

Steps to generate recommendations in R

To generate recommendations for users, we need to have datasets in a special format that can be read by the algorithm. Here, we will use the collaborative filtering algorithm for generating the recommendations rather than content-based algorithms. Hence, we will need the user's rating information for the available item sets. So, the small.csv dataset is given in the format user ID, item ID, item's ratings.

```
# user ID, item ID, item's rating
1,          101,      5.0
1,          102,      3.0
1,          103,      2.5
2,          101,      2.0
2,          102,      2.5
2,          103,      5.0
2,          104,      2.0
3,          101,      2.0
3,          104,      4.0
3,          105,      4.5
3,          107,      5.0
4,          101,      5.0
4,          103,      3.0
4,          104,      4.5
4,          106,      4.0
5,          101,      4.0
5,          102,      3.0
5,          103,      2.0
5,          104,      4.0
5,          105,      3.5
5,          106,      4.0
```

The preceding code and datasets are reproduced from the book *Mahout in Action, Robin Anil, Ellen Friedman, Ted Dunning,* and *Sean Owen, Manning Publications* and the website is http://www.fens.me/.

Recommendations can be derived from the matrix-factorization technique as follows:

```
Co-occurrence matrix * scoring matrix = Recommended Results
```

To generate the recommenders, we will follow the given steps:

1. Computing the co-occurrence matrix.
2. Establishing the user-scoring matrix.
3. Generating recommendations.

From the next section, we will see technical details for performing the preceding steps.

1. In the first section, computing the co-occurrence matrix, we will be able to identify the co-occurred item sets given in the dataset. In simple words, we can call it counting the pair of items from the given dataset.

```
# Quote plyr package
library (plyr)

# Read dataset
train <-read.csv (file = "small.csv", header = FALSE)
names (train) <-c ("user", "item", "pref")

# Calculated User Lists
usersUnique <-function () {
  users <-unique (train $ user)
  users [order (users)]
}

# Calculation Method Product List
itemsUnique <-function () {
  items <-unique (train $ item)
  items [order (items)]
}

# Derive unique User Lists
users <-usersUnique ()

# Product List
items <-itemsUnique ()


# Establish Product List Index
index <-function (x) which (items %in% x)
data<-ddply(train,.(user,item,pref),summarize,idx=index(item))

# Co-occurrence matrix
Co-occurrence <-function (data) {
  n <-length (items)
  co <-matrix (rep (0, n * n), nrow = n)
  for (u in users) {
```

```
        idx <-index (data $ item [which(data$user == u)])
        m <-merge (idx, idx)
        for (i in 1: nrow (m)) {
          co [m$x[i], m$y[i]] = co[m$x[i], m$y[i]]+1
        }
      }
  return (co)
}


# Generate co-occurrence matrix
co <-co-occurrence (data)
```

2. To establish the user-scoring matrix based on the user's rating information, the user-item rating matrix can be generated for users.

```
# Recommendation algorithm
recommend <-function (udata = udata, co = coMatrix, num = 0) {
  n <- length(items)

  # All of pref
  pref <- rep (0, n)
  pref[udata$idx] <-udata$pref

  # User Rating Matrix
  userx <- matrix(pref, nrow = n)

  # Scoring matrix co-occurrence matrix *
  r <- co %*% userx

  # Recommended Sort
  r[udata$idx] <-0
  idx <-order(r, decreasing = TRUE)
  topn <-data.frame (user = rep(udata$user[1], length(idx)), item
= items[idx], val = r[idx])

  # Recommended results take months before the num
  if (num> 0) {
    topn <-head (topn, num)
  }

  # Recommended results take months before the num
  if (num> 0) {
    topn <-head (topn, num)
  }

  # Back to results
  return (topn)
}
```

3. Finally, the recommendations as output can be generated by the product operations of both matrix items: co-occurrence matrix and user's scoring matrix.

```
# initializing dataframe for recommendations storage
recommendation<-data.frame()

# Generating recommendations for all of the users
for(i in 1:length(users)){
   udata<-data[which(data$user==users[i]),]
   recommendation<-rbind(recommendation,recommend(udata,co,0))
}
```

 Generating recommendations via **Myrrix** and R interface is quite easy. For more information, refer to https://github.com/jwijffels/ Myrrix-R-interface.

Generating recommendations with R and Hadoop

To generate recommendations with R and Hadoop, we need to develop an algorithm that will be able to run and perform data processing in a parallel manner. This can be implemented using Mappers and Reducers. A very interesting part of this section is how we can use R and Hadoop together to generate recommendations from big datasets.

So, here are the steps that are similar to generating recommendations with R, but translating them to the Mapper and Reducer paradigms is a little tricky:

1. Establishing the co-occurrence matrix items.
2. Establishing the user scoring matrix to articles.
3. Generating recommendations.

We will use the same concepts as our previous operation with R to generate recommendations with R and Hadoop. But in this case, we need to use a key-value paradigm as it's the base of parallel operations. Therefore, every function will be implemented by considering the key-value paradigm.

1. In the first section, establishment of the co-occurrence matrix items, we will establish co-occurrence items in steps: grouped by user, locate each user-selected items appearing alone counting, and counting in pairs.

```
# Load rmr2 package
library (rmr2)

# Input Data File
train <-read.csv (file = "small.csv", header = FALSE)
names (train) <-c ("user", "item", "pref")

# Use the hadoop rmr format, hadoop is the default setting.
rmr.options (backend = 'hadoop')

# The data set into HDFS
train.hdfs = to.dfs (keyval (train$user, train))

# see the data from hdfs
from.dfs (train.hdfs)
```

The key points to note are:

- ◦ train.mr: This is the MapReduce job's key-value paradigm information
- ◦ **key**: This is the list of items vector
- ◦ **value**: This is the item combination vector

```
# MapReduce job 1 for co-occurrence matrix items
train.mr <-mapreduce (
  train.hdfs,
  map = function (k, v) {
    keyval (k, v$item)
  }

# for identification of co-occurrence items
  , Reduce = function (k, v) {
    m <-merge (v, v)
    keyval (m$x, m$y)
  }
)
```

The co-occurrence matrix items will be combined to count them.

To define a MapReduce job, `step2.mr` is used for calculating the frequency of the combinations of items.

- ◦ `Step2.mr`: This is the MapReduce job's key value paradigm information
- ◦ **key**: This is the list of items vector
- ◦ **value**: This is the co-occurrence matrix dataframe value (`item`, `item`, `Freq`)

```
# MapReduce function for calculating the frequency of the
combinations of the items.
step2.mr <-mapreduce (
  train.mr,

  map = function (k, v) {
    d <-data.frame (k, v)
    d2 <-ddply (d,. (k, v), count)

    key <- d2$k
    val <- d2
    keyval (key, val)
  }
)


# loading data from HDFS
from.dfs(step2.mr)
```

2. To establish the user-scoring matrix to articles, let us define the `Train2.mr` MapReduce job.

```
# MapReduce job for establish user scoring matrix to articles

train2.mr <-mapreduce (
  train.hdfs,
  map = function(k, v) {
      df <- v

# key as item
    key <-df $ item

# value as [item, user pref]
    val <-data.frame (item = df$item, user = df$user, pref =
df$pref)
```

```
# emitting (key, value)pairs
   keyval(key, val)
  }
)
```

```
# loading data from HDFS
from.dfs(train2.mr)
```

- ○ `Train2.mr`: This is the MapReduce job's key value paradigm information
- ○ **key**: This is the list of items
- ○ **value**: This is the value of the user goods scoring matrix

The following is the consolidation and co-occurrence scoring matrix:

```
# Running equi joining two data - step2.mr and train2.mr
eq.hdfs <-equijoin (
  left.input = step2.mr,
  right.input = train2.mr,
  map.left = function (k, v) {
    keyval (k, v)
  },
  map.right = function (k, v) {
    keyval (k, v)
  },
  outer = c ("left")
)
```

```
# loading data from HDFS
from.dfs (eq.hdfs)
```

- ○ `eq.hdfs`: This is the MapReduce job's key value paradigm information
- ○ **key**: The key here is null
- ○ **value**: This is the merged dataframe value

3. In the section of generating recommendations, we will obtain the recommended list of results.

```
# MapReduce job to obtain recommended list of result from
equijoined data
cal.mr <-mapreduce (
  input = eq.hdfs,

  map = function (k, v) {
    val <-v
    na <-is.na (v$user.r)
    if (length (which(na))> 0) val <-v [-which (is.na (v $
user.r)),]
    keyval (val$kl, val)
  }
  , Reduce = function (k, v) {
    val <-ddply (v,. (kl, vl, user.r), summarize, v = freq.l *
pref.r)
    keyval (val $ kl, val)
  }
)


# loading data from HDFS
from.dfs (cal.mr)
```

  ° `Cal.mr`: This is the MapReduce job's key value paradigm information

  ° **key**: This is the list of items

  ° **value**: This is the recommended result dataframe value

By defining the result for getting the list of recommended items with preference value, the sorting process will be applied on the recommendation result.

```
# MapReduce job for sorting the recommendation output
result.mr <-mapreduce (
  input = cal.mr,
  map = function (k, v) {
    keyval (v $ user.r, v)
  }
  , Reduce = function (k, v) {
    val <-ddply (v,. (user.r, vl), summarize, v = sum (v))
    val2 <-val [order (val$v, decreasing = TRUE),]
    names (val2) <-c ("user", "item", "pref")
    keyval (val2$user, val2)
  }
)
# loading data from HDFS
from.dfs (result.mr)
```

- ° `result.mr`: This is the MapReduce job's key value paradigm information
- ° **key**: This is the user ID
- ° **value**: This is the recommended outcome dataframe value

Here, we have designed the collaborative algorithms for generating item-based recommendation. Since we have tried to make it run on parallel nodes, we have focused on the Mapper and Reducer. They may not be optimal in some cases, but you can make them optimal by using the available code.

Summary

In this chapter, we learned how we can perform Big Data analytics with machine learning with the help of R and Hadoop technologies. In the next chapter, we will learn how to enrich datasets in R by integrating R to various external data sources.

7
Importing and Exporting Data from Various DBs

In this final chapter, we are going to see how data from different sources can be loaded into R for performing the data analytics operations. Here, we have considered some of the popular databases that are being used as data storage, required for performing data analytics with different applications and technologies. As we know, performing the analytics operations with R is quite easy as compared to the other analytics tools and again, it's free and open source. Since, R has available methods to use customized functions via installing R packages, many database packages are available in CRAN to perform database connection with R. Therefore, the R programming language is becoming more and more popular due to database, as well as operating system, independence.

We have specially designed this chapter to share knowledge of how data from various database systems can be loaded and used into R for performing data modeling. In this chapter, we have included several popular database examples for performing various DB operations.

We have covered various data sources that are popular and are used with R. They are as follows:

- RData
- MySQL
- Excel
- MongoDB
- SQLite
- PostgreSQL
- Hive
- HBase

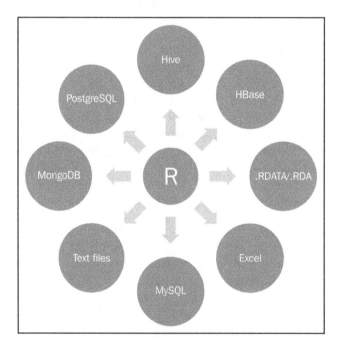

From the preceding diagram, we can understand that R is supported with several database systems to perform data analytics related operations over various databases. Since there are a large number of libraries available for R to perform the connection with various DBs, we just need to inherit them.

In the following table, the possible database systems and the related R packages are given for easy understanding of the related R packages:

Database system name	Useful R packages / function utilities
Text files	Text data files such as `.csv`, `.txt`, and `.r`
MySQL	RMySQL
Excel	Xlsx
Mongo	RMongo
SQLlite	RSQLlite
PostgreSQL	RPostgreSQL
HDFS	RHDFS
Hive	RHive
HBase	RHBase

As we know, each of the mentioned databases have their own importance with the features. Each of these data sources will be described with the following points for better understanding:

- Introduction
- Features
- Installation
- Import the data into R
- Data manipulation
- Export the data from R

In this chapter, we are going to install and interact with R packages that will be used for various data operations in R.

Now, we will start understanding about databases and how to perform data-related operations to forward to data analytics for all databases.

Learning about data files as database

While dealing with the data analytics activities, we need to do data importing, loading, or exporting functionalities all the time. Sometimes the same operations need to be iterated with R programming language. So, we can use the available R function for performing the same data activities.

Understanding different types of files

There are commonly four different types of data files used with R for data storage operations. They are as follows:

- CSV (Comma Separated Values)
- Txt (with Tab Separated Values)
- .RDATA (R's native data format)
- .rda (R's native data format)

Installing R packages

To use the data file with the format specified earlier, we don't need to install extra R packages. We just need to use the built-in functions available with R.

Importing the data into R

To perform analytics-related activities, we need to use the following functions to get the data into R:

- CSV: `read.csv()` is intended for reading the **comma separated value (CSV)** files, where the decimal point is `","`. The retrieved data will be stored into one R object, which is considered as `Dataframe`.

```
Dataframe <- read.csv("data.csv",sep=",")
```

- TXT: To retrieve the tab separated values, the `read.table()` function will be used with some important parameters and the return type of this function will be `Dataframe type`.

```
Dataframe <- read.table("data.csv", sep="\t")
```

- .RDATA: Here, the .RDATA format is used by R for storing the workspace data for a particular time period. It is considered as image file. This will store/retrieve all of the data available in the workspace.

```
load("history.RDATA")
```

- .rda: This is also R's native data format, which stores the specific data variable as per requirement.

```
load("data_variables_a_and_b.rda")
```

Exporting the data from R

To export the existing data object from R and to support data files as per requirements, we need to use the following functions:

- CSV: Write the dataframe object into the `csv` data file via the following command:

```
write.csv(mydata, "c:/mydata.csv", sep=",", row.names=FALSE)
```

- TXT: Write the data with the tab delimiters via the following command:

```
write.table(mydata, "c:/mydata.txt", sep="\t")
```

- .RDATA: To store the workspace data variables available to R session, use the following command:

```
save.image()
```

- .rda: This function is used to store specific data objects that can be reused later. Use the following code for saving them to the `.rda` files.

```
# column vector
a <- c(1,2,3)

# column vector
b <- c(2,4,6)

# saving it to R (.rda) data format
save(a, b, file=" data_variables_a_and_b.rda")
```

Understanding MySQL

MySQL is world's most popular open source database. Many of the world's largest and fastest growing organizations including Facebook, Google, Adobe, and Zappos rely on MySQL databases, to save time and money powering high-volume websites, business critical systems, and software packages.

Since both R and MySQL both are open source, they can be used for building the interactive web analytic applications. Also simple data analytics activities can be performed for existing web applications with this unique package.

To install MySQL on your Linux machine, you need to follow the given steps in sequence:

- Install MySQL
- Install RMySQL

Installing MySQL

We will see how to get MySQL installed on Linux:

```
// Updating the linux package list
sudo apt-get update

// Upgrading the updated packages
sudo apt-get dist-upgrade

//First, install the MySQL server and client packages:
sudo apt-get install mysql-server mysql-client
```

> Log in to MySQL database using the following command:
> ```
> mysql -u root -p
> ```

Installing RMySQL

Now, we have installed MySQL on our Linux machine. It's time to install RMySQL – R library from CRAN via the following R commands:

```
# to install RMySQL library
install.packages("RMySQL")

#Loading RMySQL
library(RMySQL)
```

After the RMySQL library is installed on R, perform MySQL database connection by providing the user privileges as provided in MySQL administration console:

```
mydb = dbConnect(MySQL(), user='root', password='', dbname='sample_
table', host='localhost')
```

Learning to list the tables and their structure

Now, the database connection has been done successfully. To list the available tables and their structure of data base in MySQL database, look at the following commands. To return the available tables created under mydb database, use the following command:

```
dbListTables(mydb)
```

To return a list of data fields created under the sample_table table, use the following command:

```
dbListFields(mydb, 'sample_table')
```

Importing the data into R

We know how to check MySQL tables and their fields. After identification of useful data tables, we can import them in R using the following RMySQL command. To retrieve the custom data from MySQL database as per the provided SQL query, we need to store it in an object:

```
rs = dbSendQuery(mydb, "select * from sample_table")
```

The available data-related information can be retrieved from MySQL to R via the `fetch` command as follows:

```
dataset = fetch(rs, n=-1)
```

Here, the specified parameter n = -1 is used for retrieving all pending records.

Understanding data manipulation

To perform the data operation with MySQL database, we need to fire the SQL queries. But in case of RMySQL, we can fire commands with the `dbSendQuery` function.

Creating a new table with the help of available R dataframe into MySQL database can be done with the following command:

```
dbWriteTable(mydb, name='mysql_table_name', value=data.frame.name)
```

To insert R matrix data into the existing data table in MySQL, use the following command:

```
# defining data matrix
datamatrix <- matrix(1:4, 2, 2)


# defining query to insert the data
query <- paste("INSERT INTO names VALUES(",datamatrix [1,1], ",",
datamatrix [1,2], ")")


# command for submitting the defined SQL query dbGetQuery(con, query)
```

Sometimes we need to delete a MySQL table when it is no longer of use. We can fire the following query to delete the mysql_some_table table:

```
dbSendQuery(mydb, 'drop table if exists mysql_some_table').
```

Understanding Excel

Excel is a spreadsheet application developed by Microsoft to be run on Windows and Mac OS, which has a similar function to R for performing statistical computation, graphical visualization, and data modeling. Excel is provided by Microsoft with the Microsoft Office bundle, which mainly supports `.xls` spreadsheet data file format. In case, we want to read or write to Microsoft Excel spreadsheets from within R, we can use many available R packages. But one of the popular and working R library is xlsx.

This package programmatically provides control of the Excel files using R. The high level API of this allows users to read a spread sheet of the `.xlsx` document into a `data.frame` and writing `data.frame` to a file. This package is basically developed by *Adrian A. Dragulescu.*

Installing Excel

Here, we are considering the `.xls` file as the data source, which can be built and maintained with the help of Microsoft Excel 97/2000/XP/2003.

The following are the prerequisites for the xlsx packages:

- xlsxjars
- rJava

Installing xlsxX packages:

- Install.packages("xlsxjars")
- Install.packages("rJava")
- Install.packages("xlsx")

Importing data into R

Suppose we have created one excel file and now we want to perform the data analytics related operations with R, this is the best package to load the excel file to be processed within R.

```
es <- read.xlsx("D:/ga.xlsx",1)
```

The preceding command will store the excel data with sheet 1 into the `es` dataframe format in R.

Understanding data manipulation with R and Excel

The following command will be used for selecting the subset of dataframe, `res`, which selects the first five rows:

```
r <- res[1:5,]
```

Exporting the data to Excel

As per the defined name, the processed data with the dataframe format can be stored as a `xls` file to be supported with Excel.

```
ress <- write.xlsx(r, "D:/ga1.xls")
```

Understanding MongoDB

MongoDB is a NoSQL-based distributed document data storage. This has been specially designed for providing scalable and high performance data storage solutions. In many scenarios, it can be used to replace traditional relational database or key/value data storage. The biggest feature of Mongo is its query language, which is very powerful, and its syntax is somewhat similar to object-oriented query language.

The following are the features of MongoDB:

- Set-oriented storage and easy to store the object type
- Support for dynamic queries
- Full index support
- Rich query language
- Data fragments processing order to support the expansion of the cloud level
- BSON-based file data storage
- Supported with C, C++, C#, Erlang, Haskell, Java, JavaScript, Perl, PHP, Python, Ruby, and Scala

We can use R and MongoDB together by installing the following prerequisites:

- MongoDB installation
- rmongodb installation

Installing MongoDB

The following are the steps provided for installation of MongoDB in Ubuntu 12.04 and CentOS:

First, we will see installation steps for Ubuntu.

1. Configure Package Management System (APT) using the following command:

   ```
   sudo apt-key adv --keyserverhkp://keyserver.ubuntu.com:80
   --recv 7F0CEB10
   ```

2. Create /etc/apt/sources.list.d/mongodb.list by using the following command:

   ```
   echo 'deb http://downloads-distro.mongodb.org/repo/ubuntu-upstart
   dist 10gen' | sudo tee /etc/apt/sources.list.d/mongodb.list
   ```

3. Now, update the package list of your OS using the following command:

   ```
   sudo apt-get update
   ```

4. Install the latest version of MongoDB by using the following command:

   ```
   apt-get install mongodb-10gen
   ```

Now, we will see the installation steps for CentOs.

1. Configure Package Management System (YUM).
2. Create /etc/yum.repos.d/mongodb.repo and use the following configurations:
   - For a 64-bit system use the following command:

     ```
     [mongodb]
     name=MongoDB Repository
     baseurl=http://downloads-distro.mongodb.org/repo/redhat/os/
     x86_64/
     gpgcheck=0
     enabled=1
     ```

   - For a 32-bit system use the following command:

     ```
     [mongodb]
     name=MongoDB Repository
     baseurl=http://downloads-distro.mongodb.org/repo/redhat/os/
     i686/
     gpgcheck=0
     enabled=1
     ```

3. Install Packages.

With the following command, install a stable version of MongoDB and the associated tools:

```
yum install mongo-10gen mongo-10gen-server
```

Now, you have successfully installed MongoDB.

> **Useful commands for controlling a mongodb service**
>
> To start the mongodb service we use the following command:
> ```
> sudo service mongodb start
> ```
> To stop the mongodb service we use the following command:
> ```
> sudo service mongodb stop
> ```
> To restart the mongodb service we use the following command:
> ```
> sudo service mongodb restart
> ```
> To start a Mongo console we use the following command:
> ```
> mongo
> ```

Mapping SQL to MongoDB

The following are the mappings of SQL terms to MongoDB terms for better understanding of data storage:

No.	SQL Term	MongoDB Term
1.	Database	Database
2.	Table	Collection
3.	Index	Index
4.	Row	Document
5.	Column	Field
6.	Joining	Embedding & linking

Mapping SQL to MongoQL

The following are the mapping of SQL statements to Mongo QL statements for the understanding of query development/conversion:

No.	SQL Statement	Mongo QL Statement
1.	`INSERT INTO students VALUES(1,1)`	`$db->students->insert(array("a" => 1, "b" => 1));`
2.	`SELECT a, b FROM students`	`$db->students->find(array(), array("a" => 1, "b" => 1));`
3.	`SELECT * FROM students WHERE age < 15`	`$db->students->find(array("age" => array('$lt' => 15)));`
4.	`UPDATE students SET a=1 WHERE b='q'`	`$db->students->update(array("b" => "q"), array('$set' => array("a" => 1)));`
5.	`DELETE FROM students WHERE name="siddharth"`	`$db->students->remove(array("name" => " siddharth"));`

Installing rmongodb

To use MongoDB within R, we need to have installed R with the rmongodb library. We can install rmongodb from CRAN via the following command:

```
# installing library rmongodb in R
install.packages (rmongodb)
```

Importing the data into R

We have learned how to install MongoDB in Ubuntu 12.04. Now, we can perform all the necessary operations on our data. In this section, we are going to learn how Mongo data can be handled and imported in R for data analytics activity. For loading the library we use the following command:

```
# loading the library of rmongodb
library (rmongodb)

Mongo connection establishment
mongo <-mongo.create ()
```

Check whether the normal series
```
mongo.is.connected (mongo)
```

Create a BSON object cache
```
buf <- mongo.bson.buffer.create ()
```

Add element to the object buf
```
mongo.bson.buffer.append (buf, "name", "Echo")
```

Objects of the `mongo.bson` class are used to store BSON documents. BSON is the form that MongoDB uses to store documents in its database. MongoDB network traffic also uses BSON messages:

```
b <- mongo.bson.from.list(list(name="Fred", age=29, city="Boston"))
  iter <- mongo.bson.iterator.create(b)  # b is of class "mongo.bson"
  while (mongo.bson.iterator.next(iter))
  print(mongo.bson.iterator.value(iter))
```

Understanding data manipulation

We will now see how Mongo data object can be operated within R:

```
# To check whether mongo is connected or not in R.
if (mongo.is.connected(mongo)) {
  ns <- "test.people"

#Returns a fresh mongo.bson.buffer object ready to have data
#appended onto it in R.
  buf <- mongo.bson.buffer.create()
  mongo.bson.buffer.append(buf, "name", "Joe")
  criteria <- mongo.bson.from.buffer(buf)


# mongo.bson.buffer objects are used to build mongo.bson objects.
  buf <- mongo.bson.buffer.create()

  mongo.bson.buffer.start.object(buf, "inc")
  mongo.bson.buffer.append(buf, "age", 1L)
  mongo.bson.buffer.finish.object(buf)
  objNew <- mongo.bson.from.buffer(buf)
  # increment the age field of the first record   matching name "Joe"
  mongo.update(mongo, ns, criteria, objNew)

# mongo.bson.buffer objects are used to build mongo.bson objects.
  buf <- mongo.bson.buffer.create()
  mongo.bson.buffer.append(buf, "name", "Jeff")
  criteria <- mongo.bson.from.buffer(buf)
```

```
# mongo.bson.buffer objects are used to build mongo.bson objects.
    buf <- mongo.bson.buffer.create()
    mongo.bson.buffer.append(buf, "name", "Jeff")
    mongo.bson.buffer.append(buf, "age", 27L)
    objNew <- mongo.bson.from.buffer(buf)
    # update the entire record to { name: "Jeff", age: 27 }
    # where name equals "Jeff"
    # if such a record exists; otherwise, insert this as a new reord
    mongo.update(mongo, ns, criteria, objNew,
      mongo.update.upsert)
    # do a shorthand update:
    mongo.update(mongo, ns, list(name="John"), list(name="John",
    age=25))
}
```

Understanding SQLite

SQLite is a relational database management system developed with C programming language. SQLite is ACID compliant and implements most of the SQL standard. Unlike other database systems, SQLite doesn't have a standalone process to serve data to client applications. It's an embedded SQL database engine. SQLite system reads and writes directly to the system disk files because it's a file-based database. Related SQL database with multiple tables, indices, and views are contained there and this database file format is supported as cross-platform.

Quick understanding of ACID properties of transactions:

There are a set of properties that needs to be fulfilled to perform the transactions. They are Atomicity, Consistency, Isolation, and Durability. which are explained as follows:

- Atomicity refers to the guarantee that all the tasks of the database are performed.

- Consistency ensures that the database remains in a consistent manner throughout, similar to how it was before we started.

- Isolation refers to the requirement that other operations cannot access or see the data in an intermediate state during a transaction.

- Durability refers to the guarantee that once the user has been notified of success, the transaction will persist, and not be undone. This means it will survive system failure, and that the database system has checked the integrity constraints and won't need to abort the transaction.

Understanding features of SQLite

The following are the features of SQLite database that follows ACID properties:

- Zero configuration
- Cross-platform-supported disk format
- Faster than client-server type of database system
- Easy to use API

We will require the following prerequisites for using SQLite and R together:

- SQLite installation
- RSQLite installation

Installing SQLite

To install the SQLite database in Ubuntu, follow the given commands:

```
// install sqllite by firing the following commands
sudo apt-get purge sqlite3 sqlite3-doc libsqlite3-0
sudo apt-get autoremove
sudo apt-get install sqlite3 sqlite3-doc
```

Installing RSQLite

We can install RSQLite by following the given command:

```
# installing RSQLite library from CRAN in R
Install.packages("RSQLite")
```

Importing the data into R

We will see how to insert the data into R with the RSQLite package.

To load an installed package, we use the following command:

```
#loading the installed package
library("RSQLite")
```

With the following commands, you can connect to DB and list all tables from the database:

```
# connect to db
con <- dbConnect(SQLite(), dbname="data/first.db")

# list all tables
tables <- dbListTables(con)

# exclude sqlite_sequence (contains table information)
tables <- tables[tables != "sqlite_sequence"]
lDataFrames <- vector("list", length=length(tables))

# create a data.frame for each table
for (i in seq(along=tables)) {
  lDataFrames[[i]] <- dbGetQuery(conn=con, statement=paste("SELECT *
  FROM '", tables[[i]], "'", sep=""))
}
```

Understanding data manipulation

We can manipulate the dataset using the following commands:

```
dbBeginTransaction(con)
rs <- dbSendQuery(con, "DELETE from candidates WHERE age > 50")
Exporting the data from Rdata(USArrests)
dbWriteTable(con, "USArrests", USArrests)
```

Understanding PostgreSQL

PostgreSQL is an open source object relational database management system. PostgreSQL runs on most of the operating systems such as Linux, UNIX, and Windows. It supports text, image, sound, and video data sources. It supports programming technologies such as C, C++, Java, Python, Ruby, and Tcl.

Understanding features of PostgreSQL

The following are the features of PostgreSQL:

- Complex SQL queries
- Fully ACID complaint
- SQL subselects

We need to have installed the following prerequisites for using PostgreSQL in R:

- Installing Postgre SQL
- Installing RPostgre SQL

Installing PostgreSQL

In this section, we will learn about installing PostgreSQL.

The given commands will be followed for the installation of PostgreSQL:

```
// updating the packages list
Sudo apt-get update


// installing postgresql
sudo apt-get install postgresql postgresql-contrib


// creating postgresql user
su - postgres createuser
```

Installing RPostgreSQL

We will now see how to install and use RPostgreSQL:

```
# installing package from CRAN
install.packages(RPostgreSQL)
Importing the data into R# loading the installed package
library(RPostgreSQL)


## load the PostgreSQL driver
drv <- dbDriver("PostgreSQL")
```

```
## Open a connection
con <- dbConnect(drv, dbname="oxford")

## Submits a statement
rs <- dbSendQuery(con, "select * from student")

## fetch all elements from the result set
fetch(rs,n=-1)

## Closes the connection
dbDisconnect(con)

## Frees all the resources on the driver
dbUnloadDriver(drv)
```

With the following code, we will learn how to operate data stored at PostgreSQL from within R:

```
opendbGetQuery(con, "BEGIN TRANSACTION")
rs <- dbSendQuery(con,
"Delete * from sales as p where p.cost>10")
if(dbGetInfo(rs, what = "rowsAffected") > 250){
  warning("Rolling back transaction")
  dbRollback(con)
}else{
  dbCommit(con)
}
```

Exporting the data from R

In this section, we are going to learn how to load data, write the contents of the dataframe value into the table name specified, and remove the specified table from the database connection:

```
conn <- dbConnect("PostgreSQL", dbname = "wireless")
if(dbExistsTable(con, "frame_fuel")){
  dbRemoveTable(conn, "frame_fuel")
  dbWriteTable(conn, "frame_fuel", fuel.frame)
}
if(dbExistsTable(conn, "RESULTS")){
  dbWriteTable(conn, "RESULTS", results2000, append = T)
  else
  dbWriteTable(conn, "RESULTS", results2000)
}
```

Understanding Hive

Hive is a Hadoop-based data warehousing-like framework developed by Facebook. It allows users to fire queries in SQL, with languages like HiveQL, which are highly abstracted to Hadoop MapReduce. This allows SQL programmers with no MapReduce experience to use the warehouse and makes it easier to integrate with business intelligence and visualization tools for real-time query processing.

Understanding features of Hive

The following are the features of Hive:

- Hibernate Query Language (HQL)
- Supports UDF
- Metadata storage
- Data indexing
- Different storage type
- Hadoop integration

Prerequisites for RHive are as follows:

- Hadoop
- Hive

We assume here that our readers have already configured Hadoop; else they can learn Hadoop installation from *Chapter 1, Getting Ready to Use R and Hadoop*. As Hive will be required for running RHive, we will first see how Hive can be installed.

Installing Hive

The commands to install Hive are as follows:

```
// Downloading the hive source from apache mirror
wget http://www.motorlogy.com/apache/hive/hive-0.11.0/hive-0.11.0.tar.gz

// For extracting the hive source
tar xzvf  hive-0.11.0.tar.gz
```

Setting up Hive configurations

To setup Hive configuration, we need to update the `hive-site.xml` file with a few additions:

- Update `hive-site.xml` using the following commands:

```
<description> JDBC connect string for a JDBC metastore </
description>
</Property>

<property>
<name> javax.jdo.option.ConnectionDriverName </ name>
<value> com.mysql.jdbc.Driver </ value>
<description> Driver class name for a JDBC metastore </
description>
</Property>

<property>
<name> javax.jdo.option.ConnectionUserName </ name>
<value> hive </value>
<description> username to use against metastore database </
description>
</ Property>

<property>
<name> javax.jdo.option.ConnectionPassword </name>
<value> hive</value>
<description> password to use against metastore database </
description>
</Property>

<property>
<name> hive.metastore.warehouse.dir </ name>
<value> /user/hive/warehouse </value>
<description> location of default database for the warehouse </
description>
</Property>
```

- Update `hive-log4j.properties` by adding the following line:

```
log4j.appender.EventCounter = org.apache.hadoop.log.metrics.
EventCounter
```

- Update the environment variables by using the following command:

```
export $HIVE_HOME=/usr/local/ hive-0.11.0
```

- In HDFS, create specific directories for Hive:

```
$HADOOP_HOME/bin/ hadoop fs-mkidr /tmp
$HADOOP_HOME/bin/ hadoop fs-mkidr /user/hive/warehouse
$HADOOP_HOME/bin/ hadoop fs-chmod g+w / tmp
$HADOOP_HOME/bin/ hadoop fs-chmod g+w /user/hive/warehouse
```

 To start the hive server, the `hive --service hiveserver` command needs to be called from `HIVE_HOME`.

Installing RHive

- Install the dependant library, `rjava`, using the following commands:

```
// for setting up java configuration variables
sudo R CMD javareconf

// Installing rJava package
install.packages ("rJava")

// Installing RHive package from CRAN
install.packages("RHive")

// Loading RHive library
library("RHive")
```

Understanding RHive operations

We will see how we can load and operate over Hive datasets in R using the RHive library:

- To initialize RHive we use:

```
rhive.init ()
```

- To connect with the Hive server we use:

```
rhive.connect ("192.168.1.210")
```

- To view all tables we use:

```
rhive.list.tables ()
                tab_name
1 hive_algo_t_account
2 o_account
3 r_t_account
```

- To view the table structure we use:

```
rhive.desc.table ('o_account');
    col_name data_type comment

1 id int
2 email string
3 create_date string
```

- To execute the HQL queries we use:

```
rhive.query ("select * from o_account");
```

- To close connection to the Hive server we use:

```
rhive.close()
```

Understanding HBase

Apache HBase is a distributed Big Data store for Hadoop. This allows random, real-time, read/write access to Big Data. This is designed as a column-oriented, data-storage model, innovated after being inspired by Google Big table.

Understanding HBase features

Following are the features for HBase:

- RESTful web service with XML
- Linear and modular scalability
- Strict consistent reads and writes
- Extensible shell
- Block cache and Bloom filters for real-time queries

Pre-requisites for RHBase are as follows:

- Hadoop
- HBase
- Thrift

Here we assume that users have already configured Hadoop for their Linux machine. If anyone wishes to know how to install Hadoop on Linux, please refer to *Chapter 1, Getting Ready to Use R and Hadoop*.

Installing HBase

Following are the steps for installing HBase:

1. Download the tar file of HBase and extract it:

   ```
   wget http://apache.cs.utah.edu/hbase/stable/hbase-0.94.11.tar.gz

   tar -xzf hbase-0.94.11.tar.gz
   ```

2. Go to HBase installation directory and update the configuration files:

   ```
   cd hbase-0.94.11/

   vi conf/hbase-site.xml
   ```

3. Modify the configuration files:

   1. Update hbase-env.sh.

      ```
      ~ Vi conf / hbase-env.sh
      ```

   2. Set up the configuration for HBase:

      ```
      export JAVA_HOME = /usr/lib/jvm/java-6-sun
      export HBASE_HOME = /usr/local/hbase-0.94.11
      export HADOOP_INSTALL = /usr/local/hadoop
      export HBASE_CLASSPATH = /usr/local/hadoop/conf
      export HBASE_MANAGES_ZK = true
      ```

   3. Update hbase-site.xmlzxml:

      ```
      Vi conf / hbase-site.xml
      ```

4. Change `hbase-site.cml`, which should look like the following code:

```
<configuration>
  <property>
    <name> hbase.rootdir </name>
    <value> hdfs://master:9000/hbase </value>
  </Property>

  <property>
    <name>hbase.cluster.distributed </name>
    <value>true</value>
  </Property>

  <property>
    <name>dfs.replication </name>
    <value>1</value>
  </Property>

  <property>
    <name>hbase.zookeeper.quorum </name>
    <value>master</value>
  </Property>

  <property>
    <name>hbase.zookeeper.property.clientPort </name>
    <value>2181</value>
  </Property>

  <property>
    <name>hbase.zookeeper.property.dataDir </name>
    <value>/root/hadoop/hdata</value>
  </Property>
</ Configuration>
```

 If a separate zookeper setup is used, the configuration needs to be changed.

5. Copy the Hadoop environment configuration files and libraries.

```
Cp $HADOOP_HOME/conf/hdfs-site.xml $HBASE_HOME/conf

Cp $HADOOP_HOME/hadoop-core-1.0.3.jar $HBASE_HOME/lib

Cp $HADOOP_HOME/lib/commons-configuration-1.6.jar $HBASE_HOME/lib

Cp $HADOOP_HOME/lib/commons-collections-3.2.1.jar $HBASE_HOME/lib
```

Installing thrift

Following are the steps for installing thrift:

1. Download the thrift source from the Internet and place it to client. We will do it with Ubuntu O.S 12.04:

    ```
    get http://archive.apache.org/dist/thrift/0.8.0/thrift-0.8.0.tar.
    gz
    ```

2. To extract the downloaded `.tar.gz` file, use the following command:

    ```
    tar xzvf thrift-0.8.0.tar.gz

    cd thrift-0.8.0/
    ```

3. Compile the configuration parameters:

    ```
    ./Configure
    ```

4. Install thrift:

    ```
    Make

    Make install
    ```

> To start the HBase thrift server we need to call the following command:
>
> `$HBASE_HOME/bin/hbase-daemon.sh start`

Installing RHBase

After installing HBase , we will see how to get the RHBase library.

*   To install `rhbase` we use the following command:

    ```
    wget https://github.com/RevolutionAnalytics/rhbase/blob/master/
    build/rhbase_1.2.0.tar.gz
    ```

*   To install the downloaded package we use the following command:

    ```
    R CMD INSTALL rhbase_1.2.0.tar.gz
    ```

Importing the data into R

Once RHBase is installed, we can load the dataset in R from HBase with the help of RHBase:

- To list all tables we use:

  ```
  hb.list.tables ()
  ```

- To create a new table we use:

  ```
  hb.new.table ("student")
  ```

- To display the table structure we use:

  ```
  hb.describe.table("student_rhbase")
  ```

- To read data we use:

  ```
  hb.get ('student_rhbase', 'mary')
  ```

Understanding data manipulation

Now, we will see how to operate over the dataset of HBase from within R:

- To create the table we use:

  ```
  hb.new.table ("student_rhbase", "info")
  ```

- To insert the data we use:

  ```
  hb.insert ("student_rhbase", list (list ("mary", "info: age",
  "24")))
  ```

- To delete a sheet we use:

  ```
  hb.delete.table ('student_rhbase')
  ```

Summary

In this chapter, we learned how various R packages that are integrated with various database systems and their data sets can be loaded in R to perform data analytics. Most of the popular database systems have their R packages to load the data, update, as well as query the data to analyze them.

References

In this appendix, additional resources related to the content of all chapters are presented.

R + Hadoop help materials

- Big Data university

    ° Name: Big Data university

    ° URL: `http://bigdatauniversity.com/`

    ° Type: Online course

    ° For: Hadoop and its components

- Online Coursera courses for machine learning

    ° Name: Machine learning

    ° URL: `https://www.coursera.org/course/ml`

    ° Type: Online Coursera course

    ° By: Dr. Andrew Ng

    ° For: Hadoop and its components

- Online Coursera courses for introduction to Data Science

    ° Name: Introduction to Data Science

    ° URL: `https://www.coursera.org/course/datasci`

    ° Type: Online Coursera course

    ° By: Dr. Bill Howe

    ° For: Learning data manipulation and analytics

- RHadoop
  - Name: RHadoop
  - URL: `https://github.com/RevolutionAnalytics/RHadoop/`
  - Type: RHadoop reference
  - For: RHadoop packages downloads

- RHIPE
  - Name: RHIPE
  - URL: `http://www.datadr.org/`
  - Type: RHIPE reference
  - For: RHIPE packages downloads

- HadoopStreaming
  - Name: HadoopStreaming
  - URL: `http://cran.r-project.org/web/packages/HadoopStreaming/index.html`
  - Type: RHadoop package reference
  - For: HadoopStreaming package downloads

- R documentation
  - Name: R documentation
  - URL: `http://www.rdocumentation.org/`
  - Type: Online R dictionary
  - For: R documentation

- Revolution Analytics
  - Name: Revolution Analytics
  - URL: `http://www.revolutionanalytics.com/news-events/free-webinars/`
  - Type: On-demand webinars on R and Hadoop
  - For: Importance of R and Hadoop for business applications in large industries

R groups

- Big Data Analytics using R

    - Name: Big Data Analytics using R (Facebook group)

    - URL: `http://www.facebook.com/groups/434352233255448/`

    - Type: Facebook knowledge sharing group

Hadoop groups

- Hadoop in Action

    - Name: Hadoop in Action (Facebook group)

    - URL: `http://www.facebook.com/groups/haddopinaction/`

    - Type: Facebook knowledge sharing and business context

- Hadoop

    - Name: Hadoop (Facebook group)

    - URL: `http://www.facebook.com/groups/21410812368/`

    - Type: Facebook knowledge sharing

- Big Data Analytics using R

    - Name: Hadoop Users (LinkedIn group)

    - URL: `http://www.linkedin.com/groups/Hadoop-Users-988957`

    - Type: LinkedIn group for building professional connections as well as for business context

- Hadoop Mailing lists

    - Name: Hadoop Users (LinkedIn group)

    - URL: `http://hadoop.apache.org/mailing_lists.html`

    - Type: LinkedIn group for building professional connections as well as for business context

R + Hadoop groups

- www.fens.me by *Conan Z*, who contributed to *Chapter 6, Understanding Big Data Analysis with Machine Learning*, for recommender systems with R and Mahout, Hadoop in this book
  - ° Name: Fens.me
  - ° URL: http://blog.fens.me/
  - ° Type: Collection of blogs over R, Hadoop, its components, and other open source technologies.

Popular R contributors

- RStudio
  - ° Name: RStudio
  - ° URL: http://www.rstudio.com/
  - ° Type: Software, education, and services for the R community
  - ° Contribution: Rstudio IDE, plyr, Shiny, RPubs, and devtools

- R-Bloggers
  - ° Name: R-Bloggers
  - ° URL: http://www.r-bloggers.com/
  - ° Type: Software, education, and services for the R community
  - ° Contribution: R blogging portal

- Decisionstats
  - ° Name: Decisionstats
  - ° URL: http://decisionstats.com/
  - ° Type: Business analytics with R
  - ° Contribution: Business analytics

- RDataMining
  - ° Name: RDataMining
  - ° URL: http://www.rdatamining.com/
  - ° Type: Data Mining with R
  - ° Contribution: Data mining with R and machine learning, rdatamining

- *Hadley Wickham*
  - ° Name: Hadley Wickham
  - ° URL: http://had.co.nz/
  - ° Type: Data visualization and statistics with R
  - ° Contribution: ggplot2, plyr, testhat, reshape2, and R notes

Popular Hadoop contributors

- Michael Noll, who contributed to this book for Hadoop installation steps
  - ° Name: Michael Noll
  - ° URL: http://www.michael-noll.com/
  - ° Type: Big Data and Hadoop
  - ° Contribution: Developing standard installation steps and innovative projects in Hadoop and Big Data

- Revolution Analytics
  - ° Name: Revolution Analytics
  - ° URL: http://www.revolutionanalytics.com/
  - ° Type: Big Data analytics
  - ° For: Big Data analytics with R and Hadoop for big businesses (RHadoop)

- Hortonworks
  - ° Name: Hortonworks
  - ° URL: `http://hortonworks.com/`
  - ° Type: Enterprise Hadoop Solution
  - ° For: 100 percent open source and enterprise grade distribution of Hadoop, Linux, and Windows
  - ° Contribution: Windows support and YARN

- Cloudera
  - ° Name: Cloudera
  - ° URL: `http://www.cloudera.com/`
  - ° Type: Enterprise Hadoop Solution
  - ° For: 100 percent open source software for Big Data
  - ° Contribution: Sqoop

- Yahoo!
  - ° Name: Yahoo!
  - ° URL: `http://developer.yahoo.com/hadoop/`
  - ° Type: Enterprise Hadoop Solution
  - ° For: The open source software for big data
  - ° Contribution: Hadoop development was initiated by Yahoo! and OOZIE

Index

Symbols

10 MapReduce Tips
  URL 52
.jar file 56

A

ACID properties 192
Ambari 36
Apache Hadoop 1.0.3 21
Apache HBase 34
Apache Solr 35
Apache Sqoop 35
Apache Zookeeper 35
Application Programming Interface
    (API) 16
architecture, HDFS 30
architecture, MapReduce 31
architecture, RHadoop 77
architecture, RHIPE 68
artificial neural networks 162

B

Bash command 59
Big Data analytics
  performing, with machine learning 149
Big Data university
  URL 205
Bulk Synchronous Parallel (BSP) 38
business analytics
  MapReduce definitions, used 60

C

CDH
  about 25
  installing, on Ubuntu 25-27
  installing, prerequisites 25
CentOS 188
classification technique 18
client 40
close function 101
Cloudera
  URL 210
Cloudera Hadoop. *See* **CDH**
clustering
  about 18, 162, 163
  performing, with R 163
  performing, with RHadoop 163-167
cmdenv option 90
combine function 96
Combiner function 42
combiner option 90
command prompt
  Hadoop streaming job, executing from 98
  output, exploring from 99
community support, R
  increasing 17
Comprehensive R Archive Network. *See*
    CRAN
Coursera
  URL, for Data Science 205
  URL, for machine learning 205
CRAN
  about 16
  URL 16

D

Dashboard charts 117
data
  exporting, into R 183
  importing, into R 182
  loading, into HDFS 40
  preprocessing 115
data analysis 16
data analytics
  performing 115
  with Hadoop 113
  with R 113
data analytics problems
  about 117
  case study 137
  stock market change frequency,
      computing 128
  web page categorization, exploring 118
data analytics problems, case study
  data analytics, performing 141
  data, preprocessing 139
  data requirement, designing 138
  problem, identifying 137
data analytics project life cycle
  about 113, 114
  data analytics, performing 115
  data, preprocessing 115
  data requirement, designing 114
  data, visualizing 116, 117
  problem, identifying 114
data attributes, Google Analytics 119
database systems
  supported by R 179-181
data cleaning 16
data exploration 16
data files
  about 181
  data, exporting into R 183
  data, importing into R 182
  R package, installing 182
data files, types
  CSV 182
  .rda 182
  .RDATA 182
  Txt 182

data, Google Analytics
  extracting 119, 120
data mining, techniques
  classification 18
  clustering 18
  recommendation 19
  regression 18
data modeling 18, 19
DataNode 30
data operations
  performing 16, 17
data processing operations
  data analysis 16
  data cleaning 16
  data exploration 16
data requirement
  designing 114
data visualization 116, 117
dbSendQuery function 185
Decisionstats
  URL 208
deserialization 44
directory operation 84
dist.fun function 164
Distributed File System (DFS) 37
Divide and Recombine technique 65
D&R analysis 62

E

Eclipse 52
entities, Hadoop MapReduce
  listing 40
environment variables
  setting up 66, 67, 78, 79
Excel
  about 186
  data, exporting to 187
  data, importing into R 186
  data manipulation 187
  installing 186

F

file function 101
file manipulation 83
file option 90
file read/write 83

installing 195
RPostgreSQL, installing 195, 196
print() function 73, 101
problem
identifying 114
protocol buffers
installing 66
pseudo mode 20

Q

quick check package 76

R

R
about 13
clustering, performing 163
community support, increasing 17
data modeling 18, 19
data operations, performing 16, 17
features 16
Hadoop MapReduce, coding 61
Hadoop streaming job, executing from 99
installing 14, 15, 66
linear regression, performing 152
linking, with Hadoop 64
logistic regression, performing 159
output, exploring from 100
recommendation algorithms,
  generating 170-173
R and Hadoop Integrated Programming
  Environment. *See* **RHIPE**
random access memory (RAM) 19
random forest model
fitting, with RHadoop 143-146
R-Bloggers
URL 17, 208
R blogs 17
R books 17
rCharts package
about 116
URL 116
RClient 68
RDataMining
URL 209

R documentation
URL 206
recommendation algorithms
about 19, 150, 167-169
generating, in R 170-173
generating, in RHadoop 173-178
recommendation algorithms, types
item-based recommendations 168
user-based recommendations 168
Recommender() method 19
reducedebug option 90
Reduce() method 49
Reduce phase 29
attributes 49
Reducer method 43
reducer option 90
regression technique 18
remote procedure calls 44
Revolution Analytics 61, 154, 169
URL 206, 209
R function
used, in Hadoop MapReduce scripts 101
R groups 17
RHadoop
about 61, 76
architecture 77
clustering, performing 163-167
installing 77-79
linear regression, performing 154, 156
logistic regression, performing 159-161
quick check package 76
recommendation algorithms,
  generating 173-178
reference link 206
rhbase 76
rhdfs 76
rmr 76
URL 154
RHadoop example
about 79, 80
word count, identifying 81
RHadoop function
hdfs package 82
rmr package 82, 85

Thank you for buying
Big Data Analytics with R and Hadoop

About Packt Publishing

Packt, pronounced 'packed', published its first book "*Mastering phpMyAdmin for Effective MySQL Management*" in April 2004 and subsequently continued to specialize in publishing highly focused books on specific technologies and solutions.

Our books and publications share the experiences of your fellow IT professionals in adapting and customizing today's systems, applications, and frameworks. Our solution based books give you the knowledge and power to customize the software and technologies you're using to get the job done. Packt books are more specific and less general than the IT books you have seen in the past. Our unique business model allows us to bring you more focused information, giving you more of what you need to know, and less of what you don't.

Packt is a modern, yet unique publishing company, which focuses on producing quality, cutting-edge books for communities of developers, administrators, and newbies alike. For more information, please visit our website: www.packtpub.com.

About Packt Open Source

In 2010, Packt launched two new brands, Packt Open Source and Packt Enterprise, in order to continue its focus on specialization. This book is part of the Packt Open Source brand, home to books published on software built around Open Source licences, and offering information to anybody from advanced developers to budding web designers. The Open Source brand also runs Packt's Open Source Royalty Scheme, by which Packt gives a royalty to each Open Source project about whose software a book is sold.

Writing for Packt

We welcome all inquiries from people who are interested in authoring. Book proposals should be sent to author@packtpub.com. If your book idea is still at an early stage and you would like to discuss it first before writing a formal book proposal, contact us; one of our commissioning editors will get in touch with you.

We're not just looking for published authors; if you have strong technical skills but no writing experience, our experienced editors can help you develop a writing career, or simply get some additional reward for your expertise.

open source
community experience distilled

PACKT PUBLISHING

Hadoop Beginner's Guide

ISBN: 978-1-84951-730-0   Paperback: 398 pages

Learn how to crunch big data to extract meaning from the data avalanche

1. Learn tools and techniques that let you approach big data with relish and not fear

2. Shows how to build a complete infrastructure to handle your needs as your data grows

3. Hands-on examples in each chapter give the big picture while also giving direct experience

Hadoop MapReduce Cookbook

ISBN: 978-1-84951-728-7   Paperback: 300 pages

Recipes for analyzing large and complex datasets with Hadoop MapReduce

1. Learn to process large and complex data sets, starting simply, then diving in deep

2. Solve complex big data problems such as classifications, finding relationships, online marketing and recommendations

3. More than 50 Hadoop MapReduce recipes, presented in a simple and straightforward manner, with step-by-step instructions and real world examples

Please check **www.PacktPub.com** for information on our titles

Hadoop Real-World Solutions Cookbook

ISBN: 978-1-84951-912-0   Paperback: 316 pages

Realistic, simple code examples to solve problems at scale with Hadoop and related technologies

1. Solutions to common problems when working in the Hadoop environment

2. Recipes for (un)loading data, analytics, and troubleshooting

3. In-depth code examples demonstrating various analytic models, analytic solutions, and common best practices

Hadoop Operations and Cluster Management Cookbook

ISBN: 978-1-78216-516-3   Paperback: 368 pages

Over 60 recipes showing you how to design, configure, manage, monitor, and tune a Hadoop cluster

1. Hands-on recipes to configure a Hadoop cluster from bare metal hardware nodes

2. Practical and in depth explanation of cluster management commands

3. Easy-to-understand recipes for securing and monitoring a Hadoop cluster, and design considerations

4. Recipes showing you how to tune the performance of a Hadoop cluster

Please check **www.PacktPub.com** for information on our titles

www.ingramcontent.com/pod-product-compliance
Lightning Source LLC
Chambersburg PA
CBHW060547060326
40690CB00017B/3627